FEAST DAYS

FEAST DAYS

Recipes from *The Spectator*

Jennifer Paterson

Introduction by A. N. Wilson
Illustrations by Glynn Boyd Harte

EBURY PRESS
London

For Clare Asquith and Christopher Howse

This paperback edition first published in 1997 by Ebury Press

First published in the UK by John Murray (Publishers) Ltd
50 Albemarle Street, London W1X 4BD

1 3 5 7 9 10 8 6 4 2

This paperback edition first published in the United Kingdom in
1997 by Ebury Press, Random House, 20 Vauxhall Bridge Road,
London SW1V 2SA

Random House Australia (Pty) Limited
20 Alfred Street, Milsons Point, Sydney,
New South Wales 2061, Australia

Random House New Zealand Limited
18 Poland Road, Glenfield, Auckland 10, New Zealand

Random House South Africa (Pty) Limited
Endulini, 5a Jubilee Road, Parktown 2193, South Africa

Random House UK Limited Reg. No. 954009

A CIP catalogue record for this book is available from the British
Library.

ISBN 0 09 185432 6

Cover design by Martin Lovelock
Cover photograph by John Garrett © Ebury Press 1997

Printed and bound in the UK by Cox and Wyman Ltd,
Reading, Berks

INTRODUCTION

Jennifer Paterson is the best cook I know. She is unfussy, eclectic, and extremely fond of eating, and all these ingredients contribute to the success of what she prepares. Anyone who was invited to lunch at *The Spectator* in the days when she was the cook there, could be certain of eating something memorably hearty and saporific – jugged hare, stewed ox tail, *daube de boeuf à la Provençale*, roast lamb, braised tongue are all dishes of hers which I can remember eating with pleasure and gratitude; and there was a memorable fish pie during some penitential season of the Church's year.

Those lunches were not really my kind of thing, from a purely social point of view. They tended to be all-male, and I prefer mixed company, and sometimes there were simply too many hacks, interspersed with the occasional newsworthy or celebrated politician. Jennifer would always make the meals more entertaining by bobbing to and fro between the dining-room and the kitchen, and interlarding the conversation with contributions of her own, or singing snatches from her favourite American musicals. While the editor of some Sunday newspaper prosed on about the latest feud in the Street of Shame, it was comforting to hear Jennifer's stentorian voice bellow out:

> If she says your behaviour is heinous
> Kick her right up the Coriolanus.

I can remember sitting opposite Mr Enoch Powell while he discoursed upon one of his favourite themes – as it were, the American takeover of the world, or the Primacy of St Matthew's Gospel – and watching Jennifer come up behind him, tickle the top of his head and say in a baby voice – 'Coochie-coochie-coo!' He displayed no consciousness that this was happening to him, and continued to speak earnestly, his eyes ablaze with the seriousness of his own opinions.

In one of the brilliant essays in this book, she writes:

Guess what. Last week, we had the honour of having His Royal Highness the Prince of Wales to luncheon here. What an excitement! We had sniffer dogs, sniffer detectives, idiot traffic wardens who tried to stop me bringing the food in and new table napkins. What next? H.R.H. was nice as could be, visited me twice in the kitchen where I got it all wrong and called him your majesty twice in mid curtsy ...

Someone who overheard the encounter told me that the exchange actually went as follows:

Prince of Wales: What am I having for my lunch?
Jennifer: Raw fish, your majesty.

As readers can now discover for themselves, it was her appetising *Halibut cevice.*

Jennifer is one of those far-too-rare people who think that anything is good for a laugh, and she lights up any company by her refusal to take the world seriously. It is a puzzle to me why no editor, until Charles Moore took over at *The Spectator,* ever thought of asking her to write a cookery column. She is always wittily articulate when you talk to her about any particular dish, and her writing, once she was commissioned to do it, has all the immediacy of her speech.

I have no idea how the rabbit got into Easter: pagan fertility stuff or Walt Disney cuteness? Whatever the reason, my feeling is eat it.

That is a typical Paterson sentence, combining as it does religion and a merrily carnivorous approach to the table. Her rabbit stew with anchovies and capers is superb. I once cooked her some rabbit in a mustard sauce, and it was not nearly so good. She likes unexpected combinations of ingredients, just as she likes eclectic social conjunctions — rabbit and anchovy complement each other to perfection; so do hare and chocolate. And I like her trick of adding a dash of port, or some other sweetish dessert wine to salad dressing, even though this has occasionally been hated by people I have tried to please.

Jennifer herself is far from infallible, which is one of the excitements of following her receipts — as she insists on calling what most of the world calls recipes. The most glaring example of this is her famous declaration, made in *The Spectator* on 20 September 1986, 'I shall tell you the secret of the perfect poached egg.' Readers everywhere must have read these words with tremendous excitement. No more vinegary, collapsed eggs with great skeins of white whirling away into the water — for those who manfully try to poach eggs in a saucepan — and no more rubbery little 'shaped' flying saucers for those who use an egg-poacher. At last, the perfect poached egg.

Bring a frying pan of salted water to simmering point. Place an excellent egg in its shell into the water then roll it round and round whilst intoning two Our Fathers and one Hail Mary: about half a minute. Remove egg from the water with a perforated spoon, then break into the just trembling water, cover with a lid and cook for as long as you fancy. Drain well with the spoon and serve as desired. The rolling of the egg in hot water will have set the white a tiny bit so when you crack it, it retains a nice shape.

After six failures, I spoke to various friends on the telephone who were also trying the infallible Paterson method of poaching an egg. Each had met with unrelieved disaster. The rolling of the egg in hot water actually makes the white harden slightly on the outside, leaving the inner albumen gooey and gluey. If you crack the egg open after half a minute, you will find that the outer bits of white tend to stick to the shell, or merely burst and dissolve. The inner, gooey bit of the egg splurges out in a mess.

(The only successful poached eggs I have ever cooked have been by (a) breaking the egg into a whirlpool of boiling salted water – but this only works once in a blue moon – or (b) poaching the egg in milk and water, in the same pan as some finnan haddock. Not being a chemist, I don't know why this should work, but for some reason the white does not dissolve into tentacles if cooked in milk.)

For my money, the fact that Jennifer is capable of peddling falsehoods such as her 'perfect poached egg' makes her a much more entertaining cookery writer. (And for all I know, it works for her; perhaps her Hail Mary is heard in the right quarter – hers would be if anyone's was.) These are not receipts to be followed absolutely slavishly in the manner of 'painting by numbers'. She addresses her readers, as she addresses her friends and acquaintances in real life with humorous directness, telling you her particular enthusiasms and explaining things (*pace* what I said about her eggs) with admirable clarity and common sense. 'Clams are available now in good fishmongers but I suppose you could use cockles instead or even tinned clams which have quite a good flavour …' Jennifer is not like the (in her completely different way) admirable Delia Smith whose cookery books are designed for morons. Readers of this book are supposed to use their onions when following Jennifer's directions; adapt things as you go along. Half the fun of cooking is discovering that you like a particular dish with some added ingredient not in the receipt, or some surprise adaptation of ingredients. This is precisely the sort of thing which Jennifer likes to talk about when you meet her. And reading her is very like meeting her, because she writes in such a spontaneous way.

The clams mentioned in the last paragraph, by the way, were for *Manhattan clam chowder*. You get a hint of Jennifer's cosmopolitan range when you find her recommending *Russian pashka* to celebrate May Day, *Peking duck* for Sexagesima, and *Sulimann's pilaff* as something to eat when you have been to the Islamic exhibition at the British Museum. Not that she is unthinkingly catholic in her tastes:

> I am not really into Hun food. I don't think they really have a cuisine, what they have is a lot of good produce and 1,500 types of sausage which they eat for breakfast, lunch and dinner in one way or another. Great platters of mixed sliced sausage and cheese for breakfast; lunch tends to be their main meal with enormous casseroles incorporating more sausage and knuckles of pork or veal; then, in the evening, more cold cuts with salads, soups, dumplings and potato dishes followed by some rich tart or pudding.

This does not stop her giving us two German dishes, both excellent.

Catholic, Big C, she certainly is. There's no escaping that. And there seems to be no moment during the liturgical calendar which does not call forth her gastronomic response, whether it is the Feast of SS Peter and Paul ('a suitable day for eating the very delicious fish John Dory, otherwise known as St Peter's fish, with his finger marks left on each side'), the Feast of All Souls, which inspires her to tell us about an Italian pud called *Osse dei morti*, Laetare Sunday, when her dishes (salmon mousse, pink poulets and nectarines) are as rosy as the priest's vestments, or the Epiphany. 'I've just been to High Mass on my motor-bike in the middle of a snow-storm, very terrifying, couldn't see much and a tendency to skid, luckily not many cars about so arrived safely and was rewarded by a glorious Mass in G by good old Schubert at the London Oratory. Home now unscathed and am about to reheat a thumping great goulash, just the thing for such a day . . .'

Like all good cooks, Jennifer delights in the changing seasons, and the chance they provide to savour the freshest ingredients available. Her summer cooking is particularly inventive and delicious − try the *Tomato summer pudding*, or the sea trout surrounded by a *Bloody Mary aspic*, or the mouth-watering *Chicken Veronica*. She also has the good cook's, and the good writer's, ability to make us rejoice in very simple things, such as the broad bean, her favourite vegetable. The chief reason that I value Jennifer as a friend is her capacity for joy. ('I am on an annual visit (to Cumberland) for the broad bean season; quite one of the best vegetables in the world, taken straight from the garden into the pot. My beloved host, Patricius Senhouse, picks everything very young, so the deliciousness of the beans cannot be overstated; they are a dream.') Good cooks enhance our pleasure in life by taking good things, like broad beans, and making them even better − as in Jennifer's

Broad bean Fitz. Her writing extends the pleasure further to a wider audience. I find these delightful gastronomic *causeries* repeatedly readable. They make me want to try my hand at cooking all the dishes I have never attempted. They make me slaver at the chops, imagining, or remembering, how delicious they are. And they make me laugh, as I hear Jennifer's voice in every sentence on the printed page. I do hope that this is the first of many such cookbooks, and that it will extend her fame beyond her many *Spectator*-reading fans.

A. N. Wilson
London, 1990

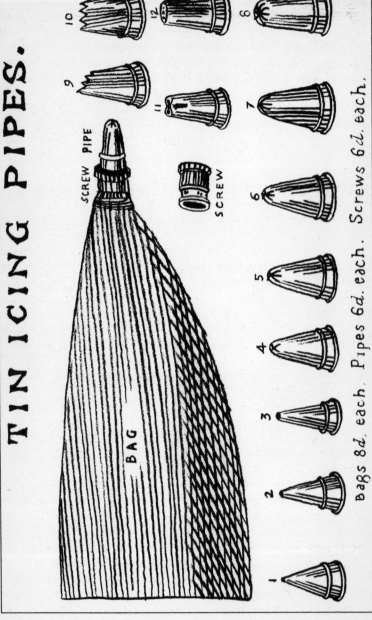

TIN ICING PIPES.

SCREW PIPE

SCREW

BAG

Bags 8d. each. Pipes 6d. each. Screws 6d. each.

Preface

I think I am the only member of my immediate family who ever willingly set foot in the kitchen. My mother had no idea of how to cook and no wish to learn, existing on gorgonzola, coffee and chocolates after the demise of any form of servant. My father having gone through two world wars was far too frightened to put on a kettle and my brothers who married young to very good wives who were excellent cooks never showed any signs of wanting to whip up something delicious for a treat; more likely retreating to toast and marmite when faced with a wifeless kitchen. I have no idea where the food bug originated in me, perhaps a far distant Viennese great, great grandparent or delicious tidbits proffered to me by my doting amah in China, who knows? The fact remains that from an early age I was to be found in the kitchen annoying the cook and concocting little messes which she kindly put in the oven for me.

I have no recollection of what we ate as children except that chicken was a great treat. Heaven knows what we existed on during the school holidays in the war. We always had a proper Sunday lunch cooked by my grandmother's faithful Rose but apart from that I think we just scavenged. The food at school was exceptionally good as we had been evacuated to Hereford and the lay-sisters who did the cooking were French or Spanish and made full use of a great kitchen garden. We always had what was called first meat and second meat, the first being a slice of roast and the second being some succulent little croquette made from yesterday's leftovers. We also had delicious risottos and pilafs unknown to the average house or school of that time.

After the war I spent two years in Berlin where the food was dicey and Naafi for the most part, with the exception of salad bowls of caviar at the Russian parties and very exciting ice-creams at the American Red

Cross. The first really good food I had was in Portugal: wonderful lobsters, fillets of beef cooked in port, great baked fishes, endless fruits and all the various *bacalhau* dishes, white truffles, tiny clams and sticky puddings. It was another world for the ill-educated taste buds which sprang to exultant life at each new experience. There were still lots of servants so one never got into the kitchen. The first time I really started to cook was in Benghazi where my youngest aunt had abducted me from Taormina in Sicily whilst holidaying at my parents' house. She was the Colonel's Lady so had to entertain a certain amount with no idea of cooking. We were lucky in having a Baby Belling – most people had paraffin stoves – and on this tiny object I had to prepare dinner parties for ten, balancing pot upon pot until it resembled the Tower of Pisa. Terrible quivering lumps of newly slain meat from the souk had to be marinated and left in the refrigerator for a week before you could stick a knife in but there were some good game birds and chickens. No fresh milk or cream, just that Carnation stuff. One of my triumphs was a dish of sweetbreads, so I thought, but they turned out to be testicles and very good they were. All in all it was a good lesson to start with; I had no real knowledge but was learning bit by bit.

The advent of the glorious Dame Elizabeth David's books was my expedition into proper cooking as for so many others of my generation and all the following ones. She was my teacher and I have never ceased to be grateful to her. The pleasure of mastering one of her more complicated dishes to the acclaim of the recipients and oneself was, and is, an immense joy.

I have had some curious cooking jobs thrown at me, all just happening rather than planned. A college at Padworth where I was enthroned as a sort of Matron at one week's notice – the real one having backed down – had been started by a friend. There was as yet no cook, so it fell to me – rather startling – my first foray into large-quantity cooking. Then a stint at a language studies establishment run by a lunatic where I had to provide lunches for the students from a kitchen the size of a shoe box: very difficult and unrewarding. Then looking after a motherless American family who all ate at different times when they (the children) weren't on drugs and never used the dining-room; an amazing eighteen months running the Uganda High Commission's flat for visiting Ugandan ministers, all of whom were very young and intent on buying gold beds and the like to take home. They seemed to like stews with a lot of thick gravy and 'Birds' custard to follow. I was finally sacked by a nasty little man (probably massacred by now) for refusing to run the place as a brothel for poor white trash, but I managed to give a lot of good parties of my own there when there were no visitors. After this I spent several happy years looking after a wealthy couple's London house where I was able to indulge in fairly extravagant cooking for their dinner parties and there were always quantities of good game as he was a very good shot. That was another good period of experimenting and learning, also it was great fun. I was living above my station in Eaton Square due to the kindness of one of my oldest friends, when I started to cook the weekly lunches for *The Spectator* due to an encounter with Geoffrey Wheatcroft at one of poor lamented Olga Deterding's parties. He told me to telephone Simon Courtauld but failed to tell Simon I was about to approach him, so our first conversation was a bit muddled but after a few hiccups it all got straightened out and I went on cooking the lunches until last year; some ten or eleven years I should think.

When Charles Moore took over as editor from Alexander Chancellor in 1984, he let me start a food column, the results of which are here before you.

A feast is a day of unusual solemnity or joy when one can delight in food that commemorates a special event. I thought it would be a good idea to attach various feasts to some of the better-known saints' days and popular festivals in the hope that the making and eating of them would be joyous rather than solemn. Makes a change from 'how to avoid cardiac arrest and food poisoning' I feel, and I hope that neither will befall you. Mine is a collection of what I would call family food which I have cooked through the years and I hope it brings you pleasure.

Jennifer Paterson

CONVERSION CHARTS

Follow either metric or imperial measurements throughout a recipe; they are not interchangeable.

Liquid

Imperial	Metric
1 tsp	5 ml
1 tbsp	15 ml
1 fl oz	25 ml
2 fl oz	50 ml
4 fl oz	125 ml
$1/4$ pt	150 ml
7 fl oz	200 ml
$1/2$ pt	300 ml
$3/4$ pt	450 ml
1 pt	600 ml
$1^1/_2$ pt	900 ml
$1^3/_4$ pt	1 litre
2 pt	1.1 litres
3 pt	1.7 litres

(1 quart = 2 pt)

Solid

Imperial	Metric
$1/2$ oz	15 g
1 oz	25 g
2 oz	55 g
3 oz	85 g
4 oz	115 g
5 oz	140 g
6 oz	175 g
7 oz	200 g
$1/2$ lb	225 g
9 oz	250 g
$3/4$ lb	350 g
14 oz	400 g
1 lb	450 g
$1^1/_2$ lb	675 g
2 lb	900 g
$2^1/_2$ lb	1.1 kg
3 lb	1.3 kg

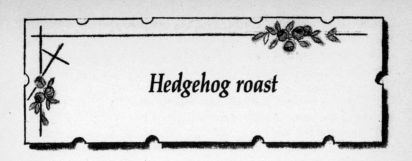

Hedgehog roast

I do not really like the description 'meat loaf', nor have I ever liked the taste of the product. It always seemed a trifle dry and sawdusty, though I am sure you have all had deliciously succulent ones.

This receipt is what I like to think of as a rather grand meat loaf that eliminates the loaf entirely. It is a good bourgeois, inexpensive dish which smells wonderful whilst cooking and is easy as pie to serve — simply carve it through in thick slices. For eight people you will need:

——— Grand meat loaf ———

1 lb each of minced beef, pork and veal
$\frac{1}{2}$ lb of chicken livers
$\frac{1}{2}$ lb of unsmoked streaky bacon
$\frac{1}{2}$ lb of mushrooms
1 large onion (grated)
10 juniper berries (crushed)

3 cloves of garlic (crushed)
salt, ground pepper, rosemary, thyme, powdered allspice, bay leaves
blanched almonds or halved walnuts (optional)
1 egg

Slice the mushrooms and the chicken livers. Sauté gently for five minutes. Leave aside to cool.

Take a large bowl and put all the minced meats into it, together with the grated onion, crushed garlic and juniper berries and a good teaspoon each of thyme and allspice, salt and about 20 turns of the pepper mill. Break the egg over it. Add the mushrooms and chicken livers. Mix together.

Place this mixture in a baking tin and mould to the shape of a hedgehog. Adorn with strips of bacon, criss-crossed Union Jack-wise, sprinkle with rosemary and place a couple of bay leaves over it. Take the almonds or walnuts and stud the roast with them standing upright to form the hedgehog shape (this is entirely optional but often pleases

1

grown-ups as well as children). You can make a nose and eyes with black olives — whole for the nose and specks for the eyes.

Place in a preheated oven at Gas mark 8, 450° F, 230° C for $\frac{1}{4}$ hour. Turn down to Gas mark 4, 350° F, 180° C and cook for $\frac{1}{4}$ hour per pound ($1\frac{1}{2}$ hours in all).

When it is cooked you will find a large quantity of juices in the bottom of the pan. Save these and refrigerate for another day. The fat will rise to the top and can be used for sautéing potatoes or bread; the delicious jelly below can be used for addition to gravy and sauces.

It is also excellent for cooking eggs in ramekins instead of the usual cream. Butter four ramekins, place an egg in each and cover with the jelly, having melted it into liquid form again. Put the ramekins into a frying pan large enough to hold them, pour hot water into the pan to come half way up the sides of the ramekins, simmer gently for three to five minutes with a cover. The eggs should not be too hard and they will go on cooking in their containers once you have removed them from the water with the aid of a perforated spoon or spatula.

But to continue. Lift the hedgehog out of the pan with a perforated spatula and place on a warmed platter. Serve with the following tomato sauce:

———— Tomato sauce ————

28 oz tin of Italian tomatoes	1 clove of crushed garlic
4 tablespoons of tomato purée	salt, pepper and a teaspoon of sugar
4 tablespoons of olive oil	chopped basil

Simmer ingredients, covered, for a good $\frac{1}{2}$ hour (more if possible — it only gets better) and finally stir in the chopped basil or, failing that, parsley.

This is a very good dish served either hot or cold. I think it is even better cold, but there is usually some left over if you are aiming at eight

AN HEDGE-HOG.

people, so you can try it both ways. A baked potato and a good salad should be ample to serve with it.

——— *Mackerel Dijonaise* ———

Now for a very much quicker dish and very good: grilled mackerel with Dijon mustard and fennel. You will need:

4 mackerel
strong Dijon mustard
3 teaspoons of fennel seed

Get fine fresh mackerel from your fishmonger (not a supermarket) and ask him to clean but not split them. Cut three deep incisions diagonally across the backbone. Salt the wounds and the inside of the fish. Spread liberally with mustard and sprinkle with well-pounded fennel seed. Heat your grill for five minutes before putting the fish under it. It is a good idea to place the fish on foil before putting it on the grid. You will then be able to throw the bones and mess away together after consuming the fish. Grill fiercely for five minutes. Turn over and put more mustard and fennel on the underside. Then grill for a further five minutes. The skin should be slightly charred and crisp. Eat with brown bread and butter followed by a green salad or a hot potato salad dressed with vinaigrette.

15 September 1984

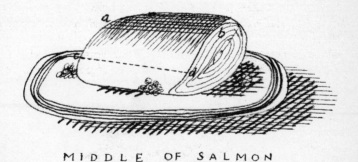

MIDDLE OF SALMON

3

Our friend Witloof

I went to a lovely party the other day all in the aid of Dutch chicory. The party was fun because all the Dutch people were so nice. A beautiful girl called Ireen gave us excellent drinks, and then we were to have a chicory luncheon — which was disastrous, as the apparently famous Chef Vogel from Amsterdam had to be left behind with a stomach ache. However, the great mounds of this vegetable piled on the sideboard bore testimony to its possibilities.

There is always a muddle in England as to which is chicory and which is endive. The chicory are the white bomb-shaped ones with green edges. Its real, glorious name is 'witloof', like a character from one of Wagner's operas. If everybody would call it witloof there wouldn't be any trouble. The endive is the tangled, curly, lettuce-type vegetable. I always thought it was the other way round, and as they both come from the Latin *cichorium*, who is to wonder?

Here are a few ways of using our friend witloof other than in the good crisp salad it makes.

——— *Witloof braised under chicken* ———

1 roasting chicken (2½–3½ lbs)	1 tablespoon chopped tarragon
6 plump witloofs	3 oz butter
1 lemon	salt and black pepper

Cut the witloofs in half longways with a stainless steel or silver knife and place cut side down in a well-buttered baking dish or an enamelled or earthenware dish. Dot all over with an ounce or so of butter and grind some salt and pepper sparingly over them. Then squeeze on the juice of half the lemon. Place in a preheated oven at Gas 4, 300° F, 150° C. Cook for 30 minutes.

While the witloofs are braising, rub the chicken all over with the other half of the lemon, squeezing some juice into the cavity. Work the rest of the butter with the tarragon and salt and pepper. Anoint the bird with this mixture and put a bit inside as well. Salt and pepper the skin and rub it in. When the vegetables have done their 30 minutes remove them from the oven, place a rack over the dish and sit the chicken on top. Return it all to the oven and raise the temperature to Gas 6, 400° F, 200° C. Cook for an hour but after half an hour turn back to Gas 4. Baste now and then with the juices collecting in the witloof dish.

When the chicken is ready, take it out and put it on a hot dish surrounded by the now succulent vegetables and all the juices. I should serve it with plain boiled rice and a tart tomato salad.

Another delicious dish is made by wrapping the witloofs in ham and smothering them in sauce Mornay. Allow two witloofs per person.

———— *Witloofs with sauce Mornay* ————

8 heads of witloofs
8 slices of ham
strong Dijon mustard

Have a good-sized saucepan full of salted boiling water. Add some lemon juice and a teaspoon of sugar. Plunge the witloofs in and boil for ten minutes. Drain well, squeezing the heads gently to extract most of the water. Roll each one up in a slice of ham liberally spread with mustard and place in a buttered dish so that they fit snugly. Make the following sauce:

2 oz butter	salt, pepper and a generous grating
2 level tablespoons of plain flour	of nutmeg
1 medium onion finely chopped	2 tablespoons each of grated
$\frac{1}{2}$ pint of good chicken stock	parmesan and grated gruyère
$\frac{1}{2}$ pint of single cream	cheese.

Melt the butter, add the chopped onion and cook gently until soft. Add the flour. Cook for a minute or so, stirring the mixture. Gradually stir in the heated stock, making a smooth paste, and then add the cream. When it has reached simmering point, turn the heat very low or put the saucepan on an asbestos mat and cook for a further 15 minutes.

Take off the heat. Stir in the two cheeses, nutmeg, salt and 20 grinds of the pepper mill. Pour the sauce over the witloofs wrapped in ham, sprinkle with fine breadcrumbs and bake in the middle of the oven for half an hour at Gas 6, 400° F, 200° C.

There's no doubt that these straight little witloofs, or chicory, are very good, with their own distinctive, slightly bitter taste. They are easy to prepare — just wipe them clean and trim off any browning leaves. Do not use an ordinary steel knife which, though it cuts best, discolours vegetables like mad. Use stainless steel or a silver fruit knife. Avoid washing your witloofs if possible but they are usually so clean that it is quite unnecessary.

13 October 1984

Nottingham Jar.

Dealing with the horny hare

The hare is a mysterious creature possessing swift-footedness, curiosity, fearfulness and Aphrodisian lasciviousness, qualities which are conspicuous in any self-respecting satyr: hence it was much admired in the good old days of gods and heroes and was meant to keep you sexually attractive for nine days after eating it. So why not have a go? I personally think it is one of the most delicious of meats whatever the superstitions, jugged, roasted, potted or what you will.

Get a young hare from your butcher or poulterer and be sure to take a suitable container with you for the blood (they never possess containers if you ask for one). The blood is important to the dish, the smell is filthy but the after-effects divine (ta, Noel). Have it jointed into eight pieces and proceed as follows:

——— Jugged hare ———

Marinade the hare with its chopped liver and heart and its blood overnight in:

1 bottle of Burgundy
$\frac{1}{4}$ pint of olive oil
2 tablespoons of brandy

10 crushed garlic cloves (crushed with a spoon not a press)
5 powdered bay leaves
3 sliced onions and the grated rind of one lemon

For the rest you need:

3 oz well-seasoned plain flour
$\frac{1}{4}$ lb unsmoked bacon diced
$\frac{1}{4}$ lb butter
$3\frac{1}{2}$ oz or a bar of chocolate Menier

2 tablespoons of tomato purée
10 crushed clove heads
$\frac{1}{2}$ lb button mushrooms
$\frac{1}{2}$ lb button onions

Dry the pieces of hare, put the flour in a plastic bag and shake each piece of hare in it to coat evenly. Fry the diced bacon in the butter gently, remove with a slotted spoon. Fry the pieces of hare until

7

browned all over, then place in a good iron casserole. Sprinkle the crushed clove heads and the bacon on top. If there is any flour left add it to the fat in the pan, cook gently until amalgamated with the fat, then pour in the marinade, bring slowly to simmering point scraping all the bits in the pan into the sauce, add the tomato purée, the chocolate broken in pieces, stir until all is melted together, season, and pour over the hare. Cover casserole tightly with foil and the lid, place in a pre-heated oven Gas 2, 300° F, 150° C, and cook for three hours. Half an hour before serving add the sautéed mushrooms and button onions and some forcemeat balls.

To make the forcemeat balls, which are well worth the effort, mix 4 oz dry white breadcrumbs with 2 oz of suet or butter, add 1 teaspoon each of grated lemon peel, parsley, thyme and oregano. Chop finely one good slice of ham, add to the mixture. Pour in a little milk and one egg to bind all together but keep it firm, add a dash of tabasco or cayenne pepper. Flour your hands and form little walnut-size balls from the mixture. Fry them in olive oil for five minutes, turning them the while, and keep ready until time to drop into the casserole.

Serve the completed dish with a good redcurrant jelly, Brussel sprouts and a purée of celeriac and potatoes (twice as much celeriac as potatoes). Instead of jugging the whole hare you can jug the legs and keep the saddle for roasting, in which case tell your butcher to leave the saddle whole. The saddle will serve two people so perhaps you could save up until you had two saddles, or buy an extra one from Sainsbury's or whoever your local is.

--------- *Roast saddle of hare: 2 methods* ---------

2 saddles of hare
8 oz unsmoked streaky bacon
½ pint sour cream

4 oz butter
3 tablespoons redcurrant jelly, black pepper

Wrap each saddle in strips of bacon, place in a snug roasting dish and cover all over with the butter. Roast in a pre-heated oven for 40 minutes, Gas 7, 425° F, 220° C. Remove saddles, place on a warm serving dish while you make the sauce. Spoon the redcurrant jelly into the roasting dish set over a low heat, stir until melting, add the sour cream, continue stirring until all is smooth, grind a liberal amount of black pepper into the delectable mess, then pour over the awaiting saddles. Carve the saddles lengthways in strips like duck. It is heavenly.

The other method starts off exactly the same until the saddles are cooked. At this point remove the bacon and pour off the fat in the pan,

Keep the saddles warm on their dish and this time pour a half pint of thick cream into the roasting pan together with 6 oz of chestnut purée, stirring again until quite smooth. Pour over the saddles and serve with all the same things as for the jugged hare.

10 November 1984

Bant a bit before stuffing

Here we are in the season of Advent, the few weeks heralding the birthday of the Christ Child and not, I would point out to the illuminationists of Regent Street, the birth of Mickey Mouse and his friends. In the Middle Ages a fast was prescribed during Advent known as 'the Christmas Lent', which like most of these dietary laws is no bad idea before all the stuffing commences, so herewith some simple but excellent, slightly abstemious fare.

—— Pasta with broccoli ——

This dish must be made with fresh broccoli; it is quite revolting with the frozen sort. It is a famous receipt from Bari where the pasta traditionally used is *orecchiette* (tiny ears) but it's fairly difficult to find here so I often use the corkscrew-shaped ones, which do very well. You need:

12 oz pasta
2 lbs flowering broccoli
5 tablespoons of the best olive oil

2 oz freshly grated pecorino cheese
black pepper

9

Fill a good-sized saucepan with about four pints of water, bring to the boil then add salt. While it is coming to the boil cut the flowerets off the broccoli stems, peel the stems and slice slantways, throw both stems and flowerets into the boiling water and cook until just tender, about five minutes. Remove the broccoli pieces with a slotted spoon or pour the whole lot through a sieve into another saucepan, thereby retaining the greenish water. This is most important as it gives the pasta the right flavour. Bring the water up to the boil again, add the pasta and cook until right consistency is achieved, anything from ten to 14 minutes. Drain and pour into a nice warm bowl, mix in the broccoli which you have kept hot somewhere, then spoon the olive oil over it, cover with a generous grinding of black pepper and maybe more salt if required, mix well with the pecorino cheese, or parmesan if you can't get the other. This is a delicious dish and couldn't be easier. You may even prefer it without the cheese.

—— Curried convent eggs ——

We used to have these eggs at school on Fridays or other meatless days. They were served perfectly simply on a bed of white rice and very good they were. I always looked forward to them. You need:

6 nearly hard-boiled eggs (7 minutes)   3 oz butter
3 medium-sized Spanish onions   1 dessert spoon of Vindaloo curry
2 level dessert spoons of plain flour   paste
$\frac{3}{4}$ pint of milk

Slice the onions as finely as possible, fry them gently in two oz of the butter until yellow and translucent. Season with salt, black pepper and a good grating of nutmeg. Stir in the flour and the curry paste, then add the warmed milk little by little until it is all amalgamated into the sauce. Put over a very low heat on an asbestos (or equivalent) mat and let it simmer for 30 minutes, giving it the odd stir to prevent the bottom catching. Peel the eggs and cut them into rough quarters or slices, add them to the sauce carefully turning them over and over, and add the remaining butter. Sprinkle a handful of chopped coriander or parsley over the eggs and, like all egg dishes, serve immediately.

This dish is also excellent without the curry paste, so you can ring the changes.

Now I think we will have a slightly partier piece which you can use as a first course or a main one with the addition of something or other.

I got this receipt from Willy Merson who lives in the wilds of East Lothian and I couldn't have been more surprised. Such dainty things going on up there!

Tuna fish pâté

2 7-oz tins of tuna fish in oil
3 ripe beef tomatoes skinned
1 tin of Campbell's beef consommé (or the equivalent good stock)
3 teaspoons of powdered gelatine

½ pint of thick cream slightly whipped to thicken
1 tablespoon each of chives and parsley
lemon juice and Worcester sauce
6 hard-boiled eggs

Bring the consommé or the stock (I prefer the stock, but it must be a good jellied one) to the boil, sprinkle in the gelatine, stir like mad to be quite sure it melts completely. Leave to cool. Flake the tuna, chop the tomatoes and eggs fairly roughly, put them all in a large bowl, add the stock and fold in the whipped cream. Season with salt, pepper, the Worcester sauce and lemon juice to your own taste and finally the chopped herbs. If chives are not to be had, use spring onions but do have one or the other. I find it makes a great deal of difference. Pour the whole mixture into a 2½ pint capacity container and refrigerate overnight.

8 December 1984

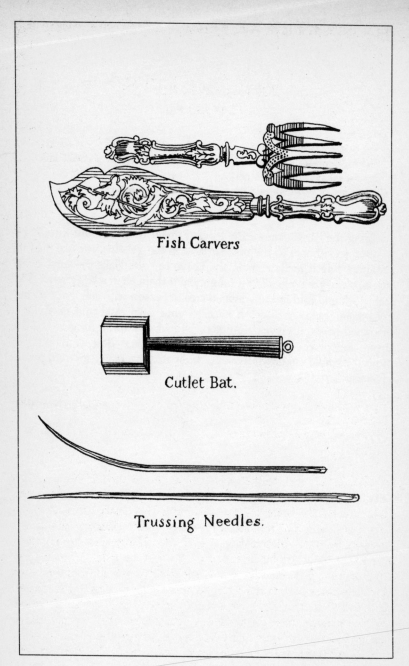

Fish Carvers

Cutlet Bat.

Trussing Needles.

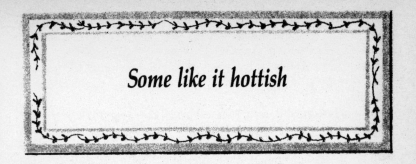

Some like it hottish

It is the Epiphany today as I am writing. I've just been to High Mass on my motor-bike in the middle of a snowstorm, very terrifying, couldn't see much and a tendency to skid, luckily not many cars about so arrived safely and was rewarded by a glorious Mass in G by good old Schubert at the London Oratory. Home now unscathed and am about to reheat a thumping great goulash, just the thing for such a day. Here it is.

Tokay goulash

2 lbs leg of pork (or shoulder)
1 tin 14 oz Italian tomatoes (more flavour than fresh)
1 lb onions
1 green pepper (capsicum not chilli)
3 oz lard or good dripping
$\frac{1}{2}$ oz each of hot paprika and sweet paprika

2 tablespoons of plain flour
salt
1 pint stock
6 fluid oz dry vermouth
bouquet garni and 2 cloves of garlic
$\frac{1}{2}$ pint sour cream
1 lb small potatoes (waxy ones)

Slice the onions and the green pepper, brown them in dripping in a big frying pan. Have the pork ready cut into 1½-inch cubes. Mix the flour and the two paprikas in a plastic bag, then shake the meat in the bag a little at a time to coat all the cubes evenly. Remove onions and peppers from the fat and deposit in a good heavy casserole in which the whole thing will be cooked. Turn the heat up under the frying pan to brown the meat quickly, turning the while to seal all sides. Add it to the vegetables, putting the casserole over the heat. Stir in the tomatoes, chopped garlic and vermouth, bring to simmering point, let it simmer for five minutes, then add enough stock to cover the contents, shove the bouquet garni (parsley stalks, bay leaf, thyme and four crushed juniper berries) into the middle, season with good salt, cover and put in a preheated oven at Gas 2, 320° F, 154° C for about one and a half hours or until the meat is quite tender. After an hour's cooking add the parboiled potatoes to the casserole. When ready stir in the sour cream and serve immediately; alternatively dollop the cream on the goulash when already on the plate. I rather prefer it that way, the texture is so delicious.

I should serve this dish with cabbage. Get one of those tightly wrapped pale green ones (called white) weighing from one to two pounds (or you can buy them in halves nowadays). They are so dense they would fell any amount of muggers if swung in a string bag round the head; the evidence could then be eaten like Mr Dahl's leg of lamb. Cut the cabbage in half, remove the hard core and slice fairly finely. In a saucepan melt 1 oz butter and two tablespoons of olive oil, mix in the cabbage, coating all over with the oils, also add some crushed fennel seeds or caraway unless you hate them. Stew gently for 20 minutes until it is cooked as you want it, add salt and pepper. All it needs is the occasional stir and a cover—don't add any water as it has plenty of its own.

This is a very quick egg dish for Nicholas Coleridge and other bachelors. Put a carton of potted shrimps (large or small depending on whether you have a guest) into a frying pan, melt gently, adding quarter of a pint of thick cream. Bring to a gentle bubble, then break two eggs per person into it; season with salt and a tiny powdering of cayenne pepper, cover and cook for about a minute until the whites have set. Eat with brown toast. Extremely good!

For an incredibly easy pudding which is irresistible, I think, make Spiller's Pudding, which I got from an ex-Chairman of the firm, Mike Vernon – it is not made of dog biscuits.

———— *Spiller's Pudding* ————

$1\frac{1}{2}$ lbs fresh or frozen raspberries
$\frac{1}{4}$ lb digestive biscuits
2 oz unsalted butter
$\frac{1}{4}$ lb demerara sugar
1 pint thick cream

Crush the biscuits in a plastic bag, banging them with a rolling-pin. Melt the butter, mix in the biscuits, cool, then stir in the sugar. Whip the cream very stiffly. Arrange in a nice glass bowl in layers: biscuits, raspberries, cream, in that order. Do it twice over.

12 January 1985

Not for the feast

Candlemas, the Purification, yesterday, such a lovely feast day, all children should be taken to it. I remember as a child being delighted to walk in procession with dangerous lighted candles dripping their wax to form a second skin on fingers and shoes, to be peeled off subsequently and rolled into disgusting little balls. Apparently Laurence Whistler used to put a large bowl of snowdrops in the house for Purification, a charming conceit. I can't think of any food for the feast except what my father used to call candle-grease buns, those long oblong buns covered in white icing, delicious and sticky, but I have no idea how to make such things so let us have a mousse instead.

The mousse of the egg

12 eggs	1 level dessert spoon of Worcester sauce
1 pint of aspic	anchovy essence
½ pint of thick cream	paprika
	1 tin of anchovies, parsley, black olives

Hard boil the eggs; make your pint of aspic (the only one I can find nowadays is made by Rieber, which is perfectly good for this purpose). The addition of two fluid ounces of dry vermouth instead of water to make up the pint gives an extra fillip to the taste. Peel the eggs, reserving two for garnish (put them into a bowl covered in water to prevent the olive tinge round the yolks). Separate the ten yolks from their whites and pass them through a sieve (a mouli legume is the easiest) into a large bowl. Chop the whites fairly coarsely, add to the yolks plus the Worcester sauce, anchovy essence and paprika. Whip the cream thick enough to leave a trail, not too thick or it won't mix. Pour half the aspic mixture into the eggs, then fold in the cream; maybe add a little salt to your taste.

15

I use a two-pint ring mould for this dish but any container will do. Pour about two ounces of the remaining aspic into the rinsed out mould and 'set' it in the refrigerator, then ladle the egg mixture on top. Chill for several hours or overnight, set the rest of the aspic as well. When all is ready turn out the mousse – placing in warm water is usually required here – chop up the two eggs and the now solid aspic, mingle with chopped parsley, and decorate at will including the anchovy fillets placed beguilingly in strips over the mousse. Scatter some delicious little dry black olives about and serve. If you want to ring the changes you can add a dessert spoon of curry paste to the original mixture, press it through the sieve with the yolks, otherwise it sticks in a lump and won't mix in.

As we are still in the grip of winter and likely to be so for some time I suggest you make a great stew of ox-tail; it is a wonderful dish, fragrant, rich and comforting.

——— Ox-tail stew ———

2 ox-tails
3 oz plain flour
3 oz of beef dripping or butter
15-oz can of Guinness (440 ml now!)
2 large onions
2 turnips

4 sticks of celery
6 carrots
salt, pepper and mustard
a bouquet garni of thyme, parsley and
    bay leaf
1 pint of beef stock

Ask your butcher for fresh ox-tails and have them jointed. The frozen ones are just not as succulent. Remove any large lumps of fat from the bigger pieces. Put the flour, well seasoned with salt, ground pepper and dry mustard, in a plastic bag, then shake the ox-tail pieces in the flour until all are coated evenly. Chop up all the vegetables. Melt the dripping in a large frying pan; when sizzling, brown the joints all over and deposit in a casserole, lifting them out with two forks. Fry the vegetables quickly in the dripping and add to the ox-tail. Put any remaining flour into the pan, stir well, scraping any residues together. Slowly add the Guinness (it fizzes like mad on contact with the heat), continue stirring, bring to the boil, then pour over the ox-tail. Heat the beef stock and do likewise. The joints and vegetables should be just covered with the liquid; if not, add some more stock or Guinness. Plunge the bouquet garni into the centre, cover the pot with foil and the lid, place in a low oven on a low rack Gas 1, 290° F, 143° C and cook for four hours. When ready remove the pieces of ox-tail into another container, taste and season the sauce, leave to chill overnight when all the surplus fat will solidify on top and can be removed easily. Keep and clarify the fat, which will be excellent dripping. Reassemble the sauce and meat, reheat; fling in a pound of frozen peas for the last ten minutes, the bright green globules look jolly in the dark gravy. Serve with lots of lovely mashed potatoes.

9 February 1985

Lenten layers

Here we are well into Lent, the withdrawals are withdrawing, dear Father Ignatius of the Oratory is giving us straight from the hip stuff about gin and sin, and the consumption of Perrier water at the *Spectator* is leaping and bounding. We are now down to two pitiful days of fasting and abstinence and there are very few sackcloths about. I wish we still had to abstain from meat all through Lent, terribly good for us as the health freaks never stop telling us and think how pleased all the poor fishmongers would be, they are going through a very hard time and in the country it is often impossible to find fish at all. If this is true for some of you, salt cod would be an excellent food to have in store.

A beloved friend in Portugal, one John Cobb, has just sent me a very delicious and curious recipe for salt cod, *bacalhau* as it is called there. It is really the national dish of Portugal and I believe they claim to have 365 recipes for it, one for each day of the year. I love the flavour and every form of it I have ever tasted. I hope you will: try this.

Bacalhau à moda de Pinhal Norte

2 lbs salt cod
2 lbs potatoes
2 lbs turnips
4 hard-boiled eggs

2 large onions
olive oil
black olives

You will find the salt cod in most Mediterranean delicatessens; it looks awful and smells worse but please don't be put off. Have it cut into convenient sized pieces for soaking. Soak in cold water for at least 24 hours, 36 is even better. Change the water frequently and/or leave under a dripping tap. Boil the cod in fresh water for 30 to 40 minutes or until it is flakeable. Remove the skin and any bones, flake. Peel the turnips, cut into thick slices and boil until tender; boil the potatoes in their skins, and when cooked peel and mash them fairly roughly. Slice the onions finely and fry gently in olive oil for ten minutes. Butter or oil an earthenware oven dish deep enough to hold all the ingredients. Spread half the mashed potatoes on the bottom of the dish, grind black pepper over them, pile the flaked fish on top, then the sliced turnips. Chop the hard-boiled eggs and crumble them all over the turnips, cover with the fried onions and finally with the rest of the potatoes. Pour about $\frac{1}{4}$ pint of really good fruity olive oil over the dish, dot with butter and heat thoroughly in the oven for half an hour at Gas 4, 355° F, 177° C. This is a great big wonderful family dish. I served it with spinach and black olives on the fish. Delicious and very Lenten.

Another very good meatless, and fishless for that matter, receipt for a first course is the three-bowl vegetable terrine. This I got from Julian (not just a pretty face) Barran of Sotheby's: he is an excellent and dedicated cook and this is a fun dish to make.

——— *Three-bowl vegetable terrine* ———

2 lbs of cooked spinach	nutmeg, basil, parsley
2 lbs of cooked leeks	salt and pepper
3 lbs of tomatoes	mayonnaise choron
6 eggs	

Have three kitchen bowls at the ready. Break two eggs into each bowl, beat them well. Squeeze the spinach with your hands to extract as much moisture as possible and place it in one of the bowls, then season with salt, pepper and grating of nutmeg. Do the same with the leeks (if you steam them there is far less water retained) in the second bowl, replacing the nutmeg with two tablespoons of chopped parsley. Pour boiling water over the tomatoes, leave for half a minute, then skin them, remove seeds and chop up roughly; squeeze out the juice and place the tomatoes in the last bowl, seasoning to taste and adding a tablespoon of chopped basil. Mix the contents of the three bowls individually and thoroughly. Butter a $3\frac{1}{2}$ pint terrine or loaf tin. Put half the spinach on the bottom, then gently lay the tomato mixture on top, followed by the leeks and the rest of the spinach. Cover the container with foil. Place in a baking tin with water coming half way up the terrine and bake in a low oven Gas 2, 221° F, 105° C for one and a half hours. Leave to cool completely, then refrigerate until needed.

Turn the terrine out onto a suitable dish and if liquid starts seeping out mop it up with paper kitchen towels. Serve with a slightly thinned mayonnaise choron. This is made by adding two dessert spoons of tomato paste to the finished $\frac{1}{2}$ pint of real mayonnaise and a few drops of water if it seems too thick.

9 March 1985

Easter bunnies

I have no idea how the rabbit got into Easter: pagan fertility stuff or Walt Disney cuteness? Whatever the reason, my feeling is eat it. The following receipt has the surprising addition of anchovies and is very good indeed.

——— *Rabbit with anchovies and capers* ———

4 lbs of rabbit sections
6 tablespoons of olive oil
1 pint dry white wine, or $\frac{1}{2}$ pint dry vermouth and $\frac{1}{2}$ water
juice of half a lemon
4 cloves of garlic
2 bay leaves, rosemary and parsley

1 onion, 1 large carrot, 1 stick of celery
1 red or green hot chilli chopped and pounded.
3 oz capers
4 salted anchovies or 8 fillets in oil
2 oz seasoned plain flour

Put the salted anchovies into a bowl of water to soak for 20 minutes and remove the bones, salt and leave to dry on kitchen paper. Marinate the rabbit pieces in three tablespoons of the olive oil, the wine, the lemon juice, the herbs and crushed parsley, two crushed cloves of the garlic, the vegetables sliced finely and a seasoning of ground salt and black pepper. Leave for six hours at least or overnight. Take the rabbit out of the marinade, pat dry with a cloth or paper and toss each piece in the seasoned flour. Heat the remaining oil in a good heavy frying pan; when hot throw in the pounded chilli and brown the rabbit pieces briskly. Place the rabbit in an iron casserole. Pour the marinade into the hot frying pan, bring rapidly to the boil and transfer to the casserole, cook in a preheated oven for 45 minutes to an hour (pierce for tenderness) at Gas 3, 325° F, 170° C. Chop up the anchovies, capers and the remaining garlic and simmer in a quarter-pint of the liquid from the rabbit for ten minutes then return it all to the casserole for a final amalgamation. Check seasoning and serve sprinkled with a good handful of chopped parsley. Some boiled new potatoes or fresh noodles are a good accompaniment to the dish.

Another simpler and quicker method with rabbit is:

——— *Rabbit Dijonaise* ———

4 lbs rabbit sections	$\frac{1}{2}$ pint of double cream
1 jar of strong Dijon mustard (145 grams)	$\frac{1}{4}$ pint olive oil
	salt and pepper

Place the rabbit sections in an oven dish, earthenware preferably. Season with ground salt and pepper, then pour the olive oil over the joints, turning them over to coat thoroughly. Anoint the rabbit with the mustard using a brush for distribution all over. Roast in a pre-heated oven, Gas 6, 400° F, 205° C for 45 minutes to an hour. Remove the rabbit to a warm platter. Place the oven dish over heat and pour in the cream. Let it come to bubbling point, stirring the while and scraping the juices and any little bits together. Taste for seasoning, then pour over the rabbit. Sprinkle with chopped parsley or coriander, serve with plain boiled rice and a crisp green salad.

Apart from hot cross buns, Good Friday demands a fish pie in the evening to reward you for your last fast of the year. It should be large, juicy and brown on top.

1 lb smoked haddock
1 lb white haddock or cod
6 scallops
8 oz peeled prawns
4 teaspoons of anchovy essence
1 large spanish onion

$1\frac{1}{2}$ pints of béchamel sauce ($1\frac{1}{2}$ pints milk, 3 tablespoons flour)
2 oz butter
salt, pepper and big bunch of chopped parsley
4 oz grated parmesan cheese

Put the haddock in a saucepan, cover with boiling water and simmer very gently for ten minutes, turn out into the sink, cool, skin and flake into a suitable oven dish. Melt the butter in a saucepan and stew the sliced onion slowly until transparent, add the flour to make a roux, then the warmed milk until you have a smooth béchamel sauce. Season and stir in the chopped parsley and anchovy essence. Slice the whites of the scallops in half horizontally and place them evenly over the haddock interspersed with their corals. Scatter the prawns on top, then pour the sauce over them all, easing it into sides and crevices with a spatula. Sprinkle the freshly grated parmesan cheese over the sauce, dot with butter and bake in the oven for 20 to 30 minutes until heated through and brown on top, Gas 6, 400° F, 205° C. Serve a purée of potatoes on the side, better than on top.

Have yourselves a splendid Easter and roll some fast eggs.

6 April 1985

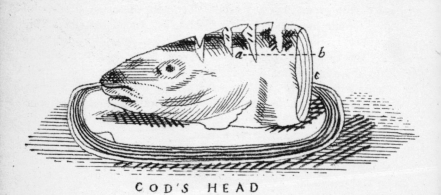

COD'S HEAD

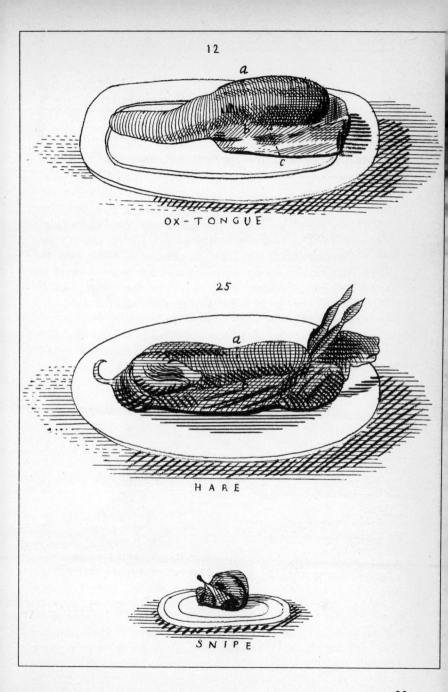

12

a

c

OX-TONGUE

25

a

HARE

SNIPE

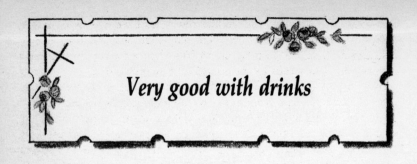

Very good with drinks

I have been to two cookbook launchings this week, both interesting and original in their own ways. The first was for Jean Conil's *Cuisine Végétarienne Française* (Thorsons) held at the Arts Club in Dover Street, London. Monsieur Conil was there, resplendent in chef's gear and bristling with medals, urging the young to become the chefs of the future. A very good idea which might reduce the dole queues and cheer up the skinheads; they could put all that energy and artful design into concocting delicious dishes. The receipts do look very tempting and are also translated into American so you can finally find out what a cup of mushrooms is. Four ounces of sliced mushrooms equals two cups of the same. Fancy!

Rice and mushroom loaf with garlic dressing

2 oz butter
2 tablespoons olive oil
1 medium onion, chopped
4 oz short-grain brown rice
4 oz sliced white mushrooms
2 oz peas
3 oz baked beans in tomato sauce
2 oz crushed peanuts
$\frac{3}{4}$ pint water
1 clove of garlic chopped
1 teaspoon each of turmeric and sea
  salt

black pepper freshly ground
sprig of thyme and a bay leaf
3 eggs beaten
2 oz natural yoghurt.

For the garlic dressing:
4 tablespoons olive oil
1 tablespoon wine vinegar
1 clove garlic chopped
sea salt and ground black pepper
$\frac{1}{2}$ tablespoon chopped parsley

Heat the butter and oil in large pan. Stir-fry the onion for a few minutes without browning. Add the rice and stir for a minute to impregnate the grains with the oils. Add the mushrooms, peas, baked beans and peanuts. Mix well. Stir in the water, garlic, turmeric and seasoning also the thyme and bay leaf. Place the dish in the oven and bake at Gas 6, 400°F, 200°C for 20 minutes until rice is cooked. Cool the rice and when cold blend in the beaten eggs and yoghurt. Transfer the mixture to an oblong terrine dish and return to the oven for 25 minutes. After cooking the terrine turn it out onto a nice dish, garnish with lettuce leaves and de-pithed orange segments and serve with the garlic dressing alongside.

I am not fond of baked beans in tomato sauce so I would substitute red kidney beans, I think. Also I hate brown rice so I would use long grain rice, preferably basmati, which has the best taste by far but would only take half the cooking time. (Brown rice never cooks in my experience.)

The other launching party was for *Traditional Jamaican Cooking* by a charming lady, Norma Benghiat (Penguin). There is a comprehensive list of UK suppliers at the back of the book and even a chapter on Medicinals and herb teas. We were offered many exciting tit-bits with wonderful names. Stamp and Go, Solomon Gundy, Manish water *á la* Norma, which turned out to be a piping hot goat broth and very good on one of the freezing May days. Stamp and Go are little fish fritters which the country people used to buy at the wayside on their travels to keep them stamping and going merrily along.

——— *Stamp and Go* ———

$\frac{1}{2}$ lb salt cod

1 lb flour

1 teaspoon baking powder (optional)

3 spring onions chopped

2 hot peppers chopped

1 chopped tomato

$\frac{1}{2}$ teaspoon thyme

oil for frying

Soak the fish in water for 30 minutes then remove bones and skin. Shred the fish finely. Place the flour and baking powder in a bowl, add the spring onions, hot peppers, tomato and thyme and just enough water to make a soft sticky batter. Mix in the shredded fish and combine thoroughly. Make fritters of the desired size by dropping the mixture from a spoon into medium hot oil and fry on both sides until golden brown. Drain on absorbent paper and serve hot. Very good with drinks.

Another very good thing with drinks instead of the usual old peanuts and crisps is the receipt for:

2 dry coconuts
salt

Break the coconut shells with a heavy blunt instrument. Cut the coconut flesh into several pieces then slice very thinly on a mandolin or with a good knife. Salt the chips, lay on a baking tray and either grill or roast in the oven turning them over as they brown.

11 May 1985

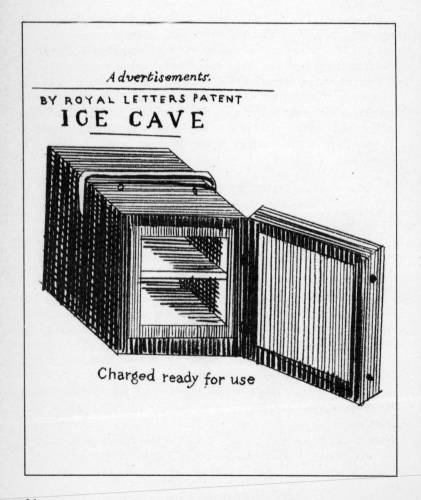

Kind hearts and crabs

I have been trying to give you this recipe since St Valentine's Day but to no avail as it always overran my allotted space, which I am unable to calculate correctly, but as the berry season will soon be upon us I'll get it in first.

Coeur à la crème

4 oz petit suisse cream cheese
¾ lb of fresh cottage cheese
¼ pint of soured cream

1 teaspoon of icing sugar
pinch of salt

Push the cottage cheese through a sieve, a mouli is the easiest method of sieving anything. Put all the other ingredients with the cottage cheese and beat well. You should have those ravishing little pierced heart moulds lined with butter muslin into which you press the mixture. Chill for a few hours, placing the hearts on a tray to catch the whey that drips out. Turn the hearts out onto a pretty platter and serve with single cream, strawberries, preferably wild but that's tricky, raspberries or stewed cherries (the tinned black ones from Bulgaria are excellent). Sprinkle with fine sugar if desired. If you do not possess the heart moulds put the whole mixture into a muslin-lined colander to drip, then serve in one mound or fashioned into one large heart by your own cunning hands.

Now for something delicious to start with. I think this is a particularly good pâté with a gutsy strong flavour and very suitable for a nice summer's luncheon.

Crab pâté

1 lb crab meat ($\frac{1}{2}$ white, $\frac{1}{2}$ brown)
4 large egg yolks
4 tablespoons of freshly grated
  parmesan cheese

4 tablespoons of thick cream
6 oz of butter
3 tablespoons of medium sherry
tabasco and lemon juice

Melt the butter in a saucepan, stir in the crab meats (you can buy frozen crab meat in half-pound packets of white and brown if you can't face the real creatures and all that difficult picking away), heat gently. Beat the egg yolks, cream and sherry together, pour into the crab mixture, continue cooking, gently stirring the while until it thickens. Add the parmesan cheese and stir until melted. Take off the heat, season with lemon juice and tabasco to your own taste. Let it cool down, give it a final stirring then pour into a soufflé dish or terrine and chill overnight or for at least six hours. Eat it on hot brown toast.
For the main course at any time:

Swedish meat balls in sour cream

1 lb each of minced veal, pork and
  beef
1 thick slice of white bread soaked in
  milk
1 egg
1 minced onion
3 tablespoons finely chopped parsley

juice and rind of half a lemon
$\frac{1}{2}$ lb mushrooms
3 tablespoons medium sherry
$\frac{1}{2}$ pint sour cream and $\frac{1}{2}$ pint of good
  stock
1 heaped tablespoon of flour
2 oz butter

Squeeze the milk out of the bread, beat the egg then combine them in a large bowl with the meats, onion, parsley, lemon juice and grated peel. Season with ground black pepper and salt. Knead gently together. Make little balls about walnut size. Sauté in butter, keep warm. Slice the mushrooms finely, cook for a few minutes in butter turning them over and over, add the sherry, when hot set light to it. Add to the meat balls. Put the 2 oz butter into the pan in which you have cooked the mushrooms, melt, then stir in the flour and cook gently for two minutes. Have the stock heated and slowly add to the roux making a sauce, then add the sour cream little by little. Simmer very slowly on an asbestos mat for 15 minutes. If it thickens too much add some more stock. Season with salt and pepper. Put the meat balls and mushrooms into a warm dish, pour the sauce over them and sprinkle with a good handful of chopped parsley and chives or any other suitable herb you have at hand. Serve with plain rice or lovely little new potatoes and a tomato salad.

The new garlic and the delectable little young turnips are here in quantity and quality at the moment, terribly pretty in purple and white. Do not miss them. Get the smallest turnips, peel them thinly with a potato peeler, quarter or slice them, then drop into boiling salted water for about five minutes, drain in a colander then finish the cooking in butter in a frying pan turning them over and over until just yellowish. Chop up a mixture of green herbs and one fresh garlic clove and stir into the turnips. This is a really good dish, the young vegetables are both juicy and slightly crisp, rather the consistency of a melon and very far removed from any dreadful memories of school turnips, so please rush out and buy some. Any excuse will do to eat the garlic, just munch it with bread!

8 June 1985

Boiled Pudding

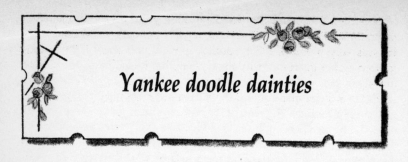

Yankee doodle dainties

As it is the Fourth of July week I think we should have a few American receipts to remind us how independent they are. We are so inundated with all those hamburger places and fried chicken joints that the real old American dishes never seem to appear anywhere. We all know about Boston; the home of the bean and the cod; but have you ever tried real Boston baked beans? I have never found them on a menu here and it is a truly great dish far removed from the ubiquitous Heinz. It takes a lot of cooking so if you have an Aga it would be the ideal stove but we who haven't can do perfectly well without.

—————— Boston baked beans ——————

1 lb small dried haricot beans
$\frac{3}{4}$ lb salted pork in a piece, or fat
 unsmoked bacon
4 oz molasses or black treacle

$\frac{1}{2}$ teaspoon dry mustard
$\frac{1}{2}$ teaspoon paprika
1 minced shallot or tiny onion

Put the beans in quite a large bowl to soak overnight or day whichever suits you best. Drain off the water, transfer the beans to a saucepan and cover with fresh water; bring to the boil and simmer gently for an hour. If you let them boil wildly they will break up and burst. Drain the beans through a sieve but keep the water they have cooked in. Place a $\frac{1}{4}$ pound piece of the pork in the bottom of an earthenware casserole, pour the beans over it. Score the rest of the pork deeply and bury it in the centre. Mix the molasses with an equal amount of the bean water, the mustard, paprika and minced onion. Pour this mixture over the beans nudging them carefully with a light spatula to let the juice penetrate to every nook and cranny. Cover the pot and bake in a slow oven Gas 1–2 300° F, 149° C for six hours. Every hour add a little of the bean water again nudging the beans gently so that the water will get to the bottom. The water should always be on a level with the beans. For the last hour of cooking remove the lid so that the top gets crispy and brown.

I once ate a terrific Gumbo Creole in Washington made by no less a person than Admiral Roscoe Schuirmann, commonly known as Pinky. He was very proud of this accomplishment, and it was very delicious in taste, full of plump prawns and oysters, but it also had a lot of okra or lady's fingers in it which spoilt it as far as I was concerned. I don't care for that slimy goo it produces, like finding boiled slugs in a cabbage, so I shall play safe with:

─────── *Manhattan clam chowder* ───────

1 dozen large clams	1 stick of celery
$\frac{1}{4}$ lb salt pork	1 green sweet pepper
1 large Spanish onion	$\frac{1}{2}$ teaspoon of thyme
1 leek	$\frac{1}{2}$ teaspoon caraway seed
2 medium potatoes	1 bay leaf
4 tomatoes skinned and chopped	2 pints of water

Clams are available now in good fishmongers but I suppose you could use cockles instead or even tinned clams which have quite a good flavour. Anyhow, put the clams in a heavy saucepan, steam them wide open over a medium heat. Cut the clams into little pieces and keep the juices from the pan. Chop the pork into little dice, cook them in a pan until the fat is melting, add the chopped onion and finely sliced leek, continue cooking until lightly browned, then add the potatoes, pepper, celery, all chopped into dice, the thyme and the bay leaf and finally the water and the clam juices. Bring to the boil then simmer gently for 30 minutes. Season with ground salt and pepper, add the clams and the caraway seed and cook for a further five minutes. Serve very hot in bowls and have some of those little hard oyster biscuits to hand.

Cranberries couldn't be more American, eaten by the Red Indians in their pemmican cakes long before the whites arrived. They are now easily found here through the good offices of the 'Ocean Spray' people. I particularly like the sharpness of their flavour and they make their own delicious sauce. This one has orange in it and is very good with ham and game as well as the old turkey.

─────── *Cranberry and orange sauce* ───────

Wash 1 lb of cranberries, put in a saucepan with 10 oz of soft brown sugar, a teaspoon of mixed spice, the juice and rind of one orange (cut the finely pared rind into thin strips). Bring gently to the boil giving it the odd stir, simmer until thick and pulpy, about 20 minutes. Leave to cool, eat at will.

6 July 1985

Here's herbs for happiness

I think tarragon is my most favourite herb, tying closely with basil. Here is a curious but very delicious receipt incorporating the former.

Panna

1 lb fresh spinach leaves
1 onion chopped finely
10 stalks of tarragon
good bunch of parsley

4 hard-boiled eggs
8 anchovy fillets
8 sardines out of a tin
4 oz of butter

Strip the leaves off the tarragon. Have a pan of boiling water ready. Throw in the spinach, onion, tarragon and parsley, blanch for five minutes. Drain through a sieve squeezing all the moisture out, then press through the sieve or put through a processor. Mash the sardines, anchovies and butter together, combine with the green purée and chopped eggs, season with ground black pepper and salt if you need it. Pack into a suitable china dish and refrigerate for at least six hours. Serve with hot brown toast and butter.

The tarragon dish I never tire of is the cold chicken sunk in a sauce of its own stock, cream and egg yolks. It is from Madam David's stable yet I rarely find it in other people's houses. It is the ideal summer dish and is best prepared the day before. Do try it.

Cold chicken with tarragon cream sauce

1 3½ lb roasting chicken
1 onion
4 carrots
1 stalk of celery
bouquet of bay leaf, parsley stalks and
  and thyme
4 tablespoons of white vermouth
  (Chambéry)

1 tablespoon of cognac
lemon juice
4 large egg yolks
¼ pint of thick cream
bunch of tarragon

Place the chicken in a snug saucepan with the carrots, onion, celery, bouquet, a squeeze of lemon juice and the vermouth. Just cover with cold water and put in a tablespoon of good salt. Bring to the boil rather gently, then simmer until tender, about three-quarters to an hour; turn it over at half-time. When cooked put it on a platter to cool then remove all the flesh in nice pieces laying them in a dainty dish which can also receive a pint and a half of sauce. Put all the bones and skin back in the liquid and simmer for a further hour thus producing a richer stock. Pour the stock through a fine sieve, refrigerate until the fat is solid on the top then remove it. Now for the sauce. Beat the egg yolks and cream together very thoroughly, take a pint of the chicken stock, bring it to the boil in a saucepan then pour over the eggs and cream stirring with a wooden spoon. Transfer this mixture to a large frying pan set on an asbestos mat over a very low flame; continue stirring until the back of the spoon retains a faint coating (as in making custard if you ever do), add some lemon juice, salt and ground pepper, the cognac and a good heaped tablespoon of tarragon. Take off the fire and let it cool a bit giving it the odd stir; we don't want scrambled eggs forming at the bottom, then pour over the chicken. Chill until set. Sprinkle some toasted almonds over the top and a few artily placed whole tarragon leaves. Good with a rice salad.

Here we are in a summerless summer in the middle of the summer pudding season, I made a beauty last week with raspberries and redcurrants but raised to great heights with a generous slurp of framboise won at the Oratory's fête, excellent! Then I thought, why not make one with tomatoes, I love tomatoes and soggy bread so here goes.

Tomato summer pudding

tomatoes

tomato passata or juice

wholemeal bread (decrusted) and sliced

garlic, basil, lemon juice, Worcester sauce, sugar

Get enough tomatoes to fill the bowl you have in mind; pour boiling water over them then skin. Chop roughly, grind salt and pepper over them and sprinkle with a tiny bit of sugar. Pour the passata or juice into a flat soup plate, season with lemon and Worcester sauce, salt and pepper. Soak the bread slices in the juice briefly and line the bowl with them. Add crushed garlic (as much as you fancy), about 20 basil leaves torn apart and a good measure of olive oil to the tomatoes and pour the lot into the bread-lined bowl. Put more soaked bread on top. Place a saucer and weights on top, leave overnight; turn out, surround with hard-boiled eggs and serve with sour cream or mayonnaise.

10 August 1985

Country matters

Things are different in the country, you have to face up to it. I have been in darkest Cumberland, was taken to a party where I asked for ice (none being offered natch) and was told by the kind and apologetic hostess that she couldn't get at it as her son had put a whole pig on top of the ice bag in the freezer. Wow! Very unusual behaviour to an urban creature like myself. However, my host with the most, Patricius Senhouse of Cockermouth, has all mod cons and is a great cook, taking delight in adding several stone to my already Buddha-like belly. This is a serious coffee pudding to lighten the heart and harden the arteries (*pace* Paul Levy) from his repertoire. They often offer two puddings in Cumberland to ensure sudden death, but seem to survive to spite the anti-everything-delicious brigade.

Pudding de Monchique

40 sponge fingers	1 oz of plain flour ⎫
6 oz of unsalted butter	1 oz butter ⎪
1 egg	$\frac{1}{4}$ pint of milk ⎬ for sauce
3 oz of caster sugar	very strong coffee ⎭
4 oz of chopped walnuts	Tia Maria
	$\frac{1}{2}$ pint of thick cream

Beat the 6 oz of butter with the sugar and egg until light and creamy, mix in the chopped walnuts. Melt the one ounce of butter in a small saucepan, stir in the flour then the milk to make a thick sauce. Cool, then add to the butter mixture a spoonful at a time, beating until smooth. Now pour in the strong coffee and Tia Maria to suit your own taste (about four tablespoons of coffee and two of the liqueur, I should think). Line an eight-inch cake tin (the sort with a collapsible bottom is easiest) with greaseproof paper and butter the sides. Dip the sponge fingers into Tia Maria and line the bottom and the sides with them. Bottom horizontal, sides vertical. Fill the cavity with alternate layers of the creamed mixture and the dipped remaining sponge fingers, finishing with a layer of the fingers. Leave in the refrigerator for at least six hours. Turn out on to a fine plate. Whip the cream stiffly, add a little sugar, more Tia Maria and coffee. Mix well together and pile on top of the pudding. Scatter the cream with coffee sugar crystals and some freshly ground coffee. YUMMO!

Now before our unfortunate summer has completely disappeared let us take advantage of the wealth of cucumbers about.

———— *Cucumber mousse with dill* ————

3 cucumbers

12 oz *fromage frais* or your favourite cream cheese

1 tablespoon of minced onion

$\frac{1}{2}$ pint good chicken stock

1 envelope of gelatine (0.4 oz, 11g)

2 dessertspoons of white wine vinegar

1 dessertspoon of castor sugar (optional)

$\frac{1}{2}$ pint thick cream

dill weed, nutmeg, salt and pepper

Grate two of the cucumbers including the peel, sprinkle with a little salt and drain for two hours, finally wringing out the moisture with your hands. In a large bowl combine the *fromage frais*, the grated cucumbers, the minced onions and the slightly whipped cream, add the vinegar and sugar. Flavour with freshly grated nutmeg, salt, pepper and a tablespoon of dill weed. Have ready the gelatine dissolved in hot chicken stock and cooled, stir thoroughly into all the ingredients. Pour the whole thing into a suitable mould, loaf tin or plastic box and leave to set in the refrigerator. Slice the remaining cucumber into very thin slices on a mandolin, salt and drain. Turn the mousse out, cover or decorate with sliced cucumber and a final scattering of dill. This looks very cool and elegant and will be plenty for ten to twelve people.

In my last piece about the tarragon receipts, my sweet editor had to cut out my warning about buying the correct sort. When you pinch the leaf it should have a strong scent and when bitten a curious taste of wintergreen, so pinch and bite before buying. I was hoist with my own petard this week due to the fact that my usual source of supply in Tachbrook Street market have all gone on holiday together, as is their wont, leaving me to purchase tarragon at some ritzy greengrocer on Pimlico Green. I didn't open the packet; I should have, it was hopeless, tasteless and my own fault, so be warned. They have the right sort in Safeways and Sainsbury when you can find it. I made the 'Panna' dish nevertheless but it was a sad affair without that special taste, though good enough according to a polite uncle. Heigh ho, we live and learn.

7 September 1985

Cooks and books

I have a little collection of cook books to bring to your attention. They seem to appear weekly: these are just a few you might be interested in. There is the huge and grand *Cuisine Naturelle*, by Anton Mosimann (Macmillan), who although one of the great chefs by any standards doesn't allow any butter, oil, cream or alcohol, which in the immortal words of the great cellist Janos Starker (I was lucky enough to be seated beside him at a Mosimann repast) is like trying to get to bed with a woman and finding no bed and no woman. Most of the receipts require the full backing of the Dorchester kitchens and its produce, I would think. Who of us mortals has six types of wild mushrooms at hand to make the curiously illustrated terrine sitting on a sinister black octagonal plate? One of the simpler receipts is the boiled veal tongue with a chive sauce, this seems quite sensible and possible, and serves four people:

——— *Boiled veal tongue with chive sauce* ———

1 veal tongue
1 sliced onion
1 small leek trimmed and sliced
1 medium carrot peeled and sliced
salt, pepper and bay leaf

Sauce:
$\frac{3}{4}$ oz chives finely cut and 8 more for garnish
4 fl oz of the tongue stock strained
8 oz fromage blanc (he makes his own)
juice of $\frac{1}{2}$ a lemon
salt, black and cayenne pepper

Wash the tongue well. Place the vegetables and bay leaf in a saucepan with the water, season with salt and ground pepper, bring to the boil. Add the tongue and simmer gently for 1½ hours until tender, skimming occasionally. Remove tongue from the stock, cool, skin and remove any fat and gristle from the root end. Return to the stock to keep warm. For the sauce, liquidise half the cut chives in the measured stock, mix in the fromage and rest of the chopped chives. Season to taste with the lemon juice, cayenne, salt and ground pepper, warm very gently. Remove tongue from the stock, carve into thin diagonal slices, and serve with the sauce, garnished with two inch pieces of chives.

There are two new books to please the more adventurous vegetarians. John Tovey's *Feast of Vegetables* (Century), which is an alphabetically arranged book of starters and main courses, quite useful when you can't think what to do with an endless supply of vegetables all coming up at the same time if you are the gardening type. Then there is Colin Spencer's *Cordon Vert* (Thorsons), which comprises 52 vegetarian gourmet dinner party menus. I would go mad if given a totally veggy meal, though he does allow eggs and good rich puddings, but all his dishes could be well used as any part of an ordinary honest to God feast.

Now we come to my two favourites. George Lang's *The Cuisine of Hungary* (Penguin). This has been out since May I think and is a perfectly splendid book with an excellent and exciting history of Hungarian food through the centuries. The receipts are mouth-watering and full of original and captivating mixtures. Scrambled eggs and calf's brains for instance, which is a traditional appetiser in Hungary. What a good idea.

Finally, Frances Bissell's *A Cook's Calendar*, a truly lovely book of seasonal menus (Hogarth Press). She is what I would describe as a cook's cook, no rot, everything in its rightful context exuding comfort, expertise from experience and creating a longing to get down and try the menus. Not much room left, so here is her stuffed squid, to serve four to five people:

--------- *Stuffed squid* ---------

16–20 squid about 5″ long
2 tablespoons olive oil
1 chopped onion, 3 cloves of garlic crushed
2 chopped tomatoes

⅛ pint dry white wine
8 oz cooked rice
salt, ground pepper, fresh coriander leaves or parsley

Rinse the squid in the sink. Pull the heads off. Cut the tentacles off and set aside. Peel the mottled skin off the body and remove the two triangular flaps, put them with the tentacles. Remove the 'backbone' from body then squeeze it to get rid of anything inside. Rinse again. Heat a tablespoon of oil in a pan, fry the onion first then add the chopped tentacles, flaps and garlic until the squid becomes opaque, then add the tomatoes, herbs, seasoning and rice. Stuff the squid bodies with this mixture, lay in a greased oven dish, pour the wine and remaining oil over, cover with foil and bake in a heated oven Gas 4, 350° F, 180° C, for ten minutes.

Serve sprinkled with fresh herbs and a salad on the side.

5 October 1985

FOUR-PRONGED BREAKER

PRICKERS

THE 'NEAPOLITAN' SOLID BRASS ICE SPOON

8s. 3d., 9s., and 9s. 9d. each.

ICE SPADDLES.

SACCHAROMETERS
FOR TESTING THE STRENGTH OF SYRUPS
3s. 6d. the box

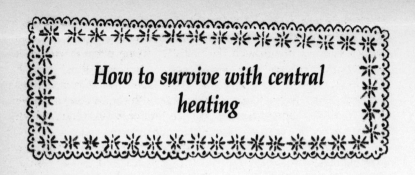

How to survive with central heating

I wouldn't like you to think that our wonderful Patrick Kavanagh is the only film star in our firmament. I too have been wandering through Tinsel City. I was roped in for the banquet scene (very appropriate, *hein*?) in Derrick Jarman's new film of Caravaggio. I was picked up at 7.30 a.m., taken to a warehouse on the Isle of Dogs, painted and primped, clad in splendid robes and ruffs, dusted down with Fuller's earth for some reason best known to the producer, remained there until 10.30 p.m. being constantly fed by a feeding van outside on the wharf and sitting around with several cardinals and courtiers; and if you blink once, I doubt you will catch a glimpse of me. It was all great fun, but Lord it does take time.

Enough of all that; winter is here, I have already got a cold owing to new central heating and my thoughts are turning to the casserole pot and lovely rich stews. Here is a very good dish:

——— Beef roulade ———

6 thin slices of beef known as beef
   olives (why?)
6 slices of unsmoked back bacon
1 large onion
2 cucumber pickles

big bunch of parsley
2 large cloves of garlic
2 tablespoons of tomato purée
12 fluid oz of burgundy
salt, pepper and plain flour

Chop the parsley and onion finely, slice the cucumber pickles lengthways to get six uniform pieces. Spread the beef olives out on a board or suitable surface, squash the garlic and anoint each piece of beef with it, rubbing it well in. Season with salt and ground black pepper. Spread the onion and parsley mixture over each slice as fairly as possible, then lay a slice of bacon and one of cucumber on each. Roll up each little parcel neatly and secure with toothpicks or cocktail sticks. Dredge with flour. Heat some bacon fat or butter or both in a large heavy frying pan, then brown the beef roulades all over. Remove from the pan and place in a snug casserole. Pour the wine into the frying pan, bring to the boil scraping any little bits left from the frying into the wine, mix in the tomato purée and pour over the meat in the casserole. Cover and place in a preheated oven at Gas 2, 310° F, 154° C. Cook for an hour or an hour and a half until quite tender. Check the seasoning and serve with some plain boiled noodles and an endive salad adorned with chopped black olives.

Parsnips are an excellent accompaniment to these winter dishes, though many were turned against them in youth. I defy any parsnip-hater not to be wooed by this method of cooking them:

Parsnip and garlic creamed purée

2 lbs of parsnips
5 cloves of garlic
2 oz butter
$\frac{1}{4}$ pint thick cream
salt and pepper

Peel the parsnips, quarter them and cut into little chunks. Have ready a saucepan of boiling salted water, throw in the garlic cloves for a few seconds, then fish them out with a slotted spoon and peel. Put the parsnips and the garlic in the boiling water, cook until tender, not long, about five to seven minutes. Strain well then pass the vegetables through a sieve or mouli, or whizz to a purée in some machine. Beat in the butter and then the cream, season with salt and ground black pepper. Spread the parsnips evenly onto a *gratin* dish, then grill briskly until you have a nice brown crust. You can do all this in advance if you wish and just heat up in the oven when desired. It's a dream.

The uncle brought home four of those little quail this week. They always remind me of that glorious Pont cartoon 'Gosh, quails in aspic again,' uttered by a despairing deb of the time.

Stuffed quail

4 quail
$\frac{1}{4}$ lb of mushrooms, chopped
$\frac{1}{4}$ lb of shallots, chopped
1 tablespoon of chopped parsley and
    2 sage leaves
4 strips of fat bacon
1 oz butter
liver pâté (optional) if you happen to
    have some
2 tablespoons of brandy

Fry the mushrooms and shallots in the butter gently until soft, mix in the parsley, season with salt, pepper and nutmeg. Stuff the birds adding a teaspoon of pâté per bird if you have it. Place birds in a small roasting tin, rinse the frying pan with a little brandy, set fire to it, then pour over the quail. Cover each little breast with a piece of bacon and roast in a preheated oven at Gas 7, 425 °F, 218 °C, for 30 minutes. Wild or tame fried rice is good with the tiny creatures.

9 November 1985

Cod, conger eel and turkey stuffing

The first Sunday in Advent already, and the first sign of sun for what seems an age, quite balmy today; but, as this is my last piece for the year, some suitable and seasonable suggestions are warranted.

My splendid John Cobb from Portugal has been over and left me with another bacalhau dish, very curious in that you bake the mayonnaise. Remember that the bacalhau (salt cod fish) must be soaked for at least 24 hours, preferably 36, with constant changes of water. This dish would be very correct for Christmas Eve before Midnight Mass. Get the thickest pieces of fish you can find.

——— Bacalhau à zé do pipo (Oporto) ———

4 thick fillets of bacalhau
1¾ pints of milk
2 medium onions
4 tablespoons of virgin olive oil

salt, pepper and bay leaf
1 bowl of mayonnaise (2 egg yolks, 12 oz olive oil)
2 lbs of potatoes

After soaking the fish, cut into the four portions and boil gently in the milk until tender when pierced (about 30 minutes). Chop the onions, cook them in olive oil with the bay leaf, ground salt and pepper and a little of the fish milk until transparent and golden. Boil the potatoes in their skins, peel and purée them. In an earthenware oven dish set the pieces of fish in the centre, surround with the puréed potato, cover the fish with the onion mixture then apply the mayonnaise on top; brown in a preheated oven for about 20 minutes at Gas 5, 380 °F, 193 °C. Serve garnished with black olives and a green salad, I should think.

Another fish you might not have tried too often is conger eel; it has delicious firm white flesh and takes much longer to cook than other white fish, but its disadvantage is in the quantity of tiny bones it contains, especially toward the tail end, so try to get a cut from behind the head. At any rate it will be simpler than having a bathful of live eels as Digby Anderson had last Christmas Eve.

———— *Braised conger eel* ————

2 lbs of conger eel
4 carrots
3 medium onions
1 sweet red pepper

1 14 oz tin chopped tomatoes
salt, pepper and nutmeg
fennel seeds or a sprig of fresh fennel
$\frac{1}{4}$ pint dry vermouth

Peel and slice the carrots finely and diagonally, chop the onions and the deseeded red pepper. Have an oval casserole with a lid which the fish will fit into, cover the base with olive oil and place the mixed chopped vegetables in an even layer over the surface. Cook over the heat until starting to brown. Place the eel on top, pour the tinned tomatoes and vermouth over it, season with salt, pepper and nutmeg, scatter some crushed fennel seeds or place a sprig of the herb on the fish, continue to cook until everything is bubbling, then cover and place in a pre-heated oven Gas 4, 355 °F, 179 °C, for about an hour until cooked. Halfway through turn the eel over and give it a good basting. Serve from the dish, having flung a generous amount of chopped parsley over all.

If you are going to have a turkey the great thing is not to overcook it, otherwise it is a dry old beast. The best way to keep it moist is to cover it in a lot of soft butter, a lot of streaky bacon, then wrap it into a large loose parcel with foil. Cook low down in the oven, high temperature for the first half-hour, then low like Gas 3 for most of the time, then for the last half-hour remove foil and bacon, turn up high again for browning. Rest the bird somewhere warm for 20 minutes before carving.

I found lovely John Patten in the lift yesterday (something to do with housing) who thinks that to stuff a goose you put a lump of coal up one end and an onion down the other. Tut tut, or maybe he's right? However, this is my most favourite stuffing for turkey, far too rich for goose anyway.

Collect together: one large cooking apple, one large onion, two fat cloves of garlic, a handful of parsley, two sage leaves, $\frac{1}{2}$ lb best quality sausage meat, $\frac{1}{2}$ lb of back bacon, $\frac{1}{2}$ lb of loin of pork with the fat (like a good chop), 6 oz of mushrooms sliced and gently fried in butter for a moment, a tin of puréed chestnuts approx. 15 oz (not the heavily sweetened one) unless you have the guts to peel the real things, the turkey liver and finally about 6 oz of some pâté de foie.

Chop everything finely, good knives or processors or what you will, season with a good deal of ground black pepper, 8 crushed juniper berries and very little salt. Mix well and stuff both ends of the bird.

And a Bon Nöel to you all.

7 December 1985

COD'S HEAD

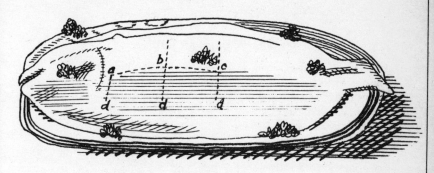

TURBOT

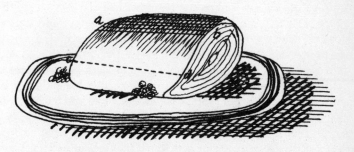

MIDDLE OF SALMON

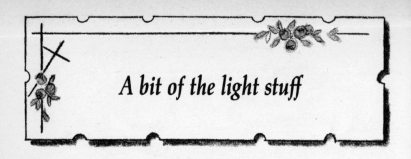

A bit of the light stuff

Should you be the proud possessor of a real larder, the heel of some great ham and the remnants of a huge potted tongue, the following receipt will be useful for polishing off the meats. Otherwise they may be purchased at will, to make this elegant and delicious cold soufflé:

——— Soufflé glacé au jambon ———

1 lb cooked lean ham
½ lb cooked tongue
1 envelope of gelatine (0.4 oz, 11 g)
¼ pint of dry vermouth
1 pint of thick cream

½ pint of good chicken stock
3 tablespoons finely chopped shallots
   or spring onions
4 egg whites
1 oz of butter, black pepper

Pour the gelatine into the vermouth and leave for a few minutes to get spongy. In a little cooking pan melt the onions in the butter for about two minutes until soft, add half the stock, bring to the boil, then simmer for another minute; take off the heat and beat in the gelatine and vermouth mixture until thoroughly dissolved. Chop the ham, then pound to a paste in a liquidiser or processor; failing both instruments you can use a pestle and mortar but it is a hell of a sweat. Add the rest of the stock to facilitate the processing. Cut the tongue into small cubes, combine with the ham paste in a large bowl, mix with the onions and gelatine. Whip the cream until it leaves a trail when dripped and fold into the ham, adding some freshly ground black pepper. Place in the refrigerator for about half an hour to stiffen a little. Whip the egg whites until stiff enough to hold soft peaks; carefully fold into the ham mixture, then pour the lot into a two-pint soufflé dish. Refrigerate for six hours or until set. Serve with a sprinkling of parsley and some hot toast. If you are using a processor be sure to put the stock in with the ham right from the start. The first time I tried this, I put the ham in alone and it whizzed itself into fine gravel.

I have no idea what the next concoction is called, it is a sort of half soufflé rather like the Italian sformato but without the bechamel. I got it years ago from Jane Barran (the Kensington Square one – there are others). It has an interesting taste and makes a good supper dish. Let's call it:

Spectator surprise soufflé

10 oz of string beans	4 oz of olive oil
1 sweet green pepper	4 eggs
1 sweet red pepper	5 oz tin of artichoke hearts (approx)
1 large onion	

The beans can be fresh or frozen. Cook them and drain well. Chop the onion and cook until soft in some of the oil. Dice the green pepper. Place the beans, artichokes, onions and the rest of the olive oil in the blender, whizz to a purée. Pour into a bowl, add the diced pepper then season with ground salt and pepper. Beat the eggs thoroughly and fold into the vegetable purée. Pour into a well buttered soufflé dish then cook in a preheated oven Gas 4, 350 °F, 177 °C, for 45 minutes. When ready, decorate the top with thin strips of the red pepper for jolliness's sake as it is a fairly sinister colour.

From the same source a wonderful way for cooking winter carrots. Pound for pound you need twice as many carrots as onions so let's say one pound of carrots to half a pound of onions. Slice both as finely as possible after peeling. Slice the carrots on the bias; not only do they look more fetching but in some strange way it's easier. Melt 2 oz of dripping or butter in a fine big frying pan, toss in the vegetables to cook until they brown a little; season with salt, ground pepper and a dusting of flour, mix well, then moisten with stock. Simmer uncovered until tender, returning to give the odd stir (takes 40 to 50 minutes). When ready, put in a dash of wine vinegar, a handful of chopped parsley and the yolk of an egg. Mix vigorously and serve.

If you are surrounded by pheasant or the happy receiver of such birds, a hint to keep them moist and succulent. Make a stuffing from a quarter-pound of good sausage meat, one stick of celery and a sweet apple. Mash all together with 2 oz of butter. This is ample for two birds. This stuffing is not for eating, but you can add it to the bones when you are making a stock. Cover the birds with good slices of pork fat until the last ten minutes and the result will never be dry.

11 January 1986

Fast food and faint hearts

We are having such an early Lent this year that St Valentine's day comes two days after Ash Wednesday, by which time we should all have started some fast or other unless you follow the dictates of health freaks, macrobiotic doctors, most of the American nation (if we believe the propaganda) and live in a perpetual limbo of Lenten lentils, brown rice and wholemeal crusts washed down by herbal teas. If on the other hand you are still into old-fashioned, delicious food and drink you will probably be giving up something alcoholic or fattening, which alcohol is for most people. Loss of weight is always nice after dutiful abstinence so if you need to trim down lay in stocks of no-calorie ginger ale and angostura bitters for cocktails, decaffeinated coffee for the evening or you won't get to sleep. Steam suitable green vegetables and onions, poach fish and chicken in good stocks of their own making, have two fruits and two Ryvitas a day, eat supper early and you will all be streamlined sveltes for Easter and terribly, terribly bored but bright-eyed and bouncy.

That said, let us have a receipt for heart to celebrate St Valentine. If you have never tried heart please do, it is very like wild duck in texture and served with a sauce Bigarade is hardly distinguishable.

———— Veal hearts Valentine ————

2 veal hearts
1 medium onion chopped
1 clove of garlic crushed
1 tablespoon chopped parsley
4 oz of chopped mushrooms
4 oz of good sausage meat
8 oz fresh bread crumbs

1 egg
salt, pepper, nutmeg and sage
3 tablespoons port or sherry
4 shallots and 4 juniper berries
streaky bacon and chicken fat
white wine and beef stock

Wash the hearts in warm water. Cut away all veins and arteries to make a nice cavity for the stuffing; soak in milk for an hour. Drain, dry well with kitchen towel then season with ground pepper, salt and nutmeg. For the stuffing, stir fry the onion, garlic and parsley in a little chicken fat for a minute, add the mushrooms and sausage meat and let them brown a little, stirring and mixing all together. Pour in the breadcrumbs, two chopped leaves of sage, season with salt and pepper. Take off the heat and moisten with the port and some beaten egg to bind all the ingredients. Stuff the hearts with this mixture, wrap each one in slices of streaky bacon and secure with toothpicks. Heat some more chicken fat in your pan and quickly brown the hearts on all sides. Place them in a snug casserole and cover with equal quantities of white wine and beef stock. Insert the shallots, the crushed juniper berries and a bouquet garni. Cover the pot and bake in a preheated oven at Gas 4, 355 °F, 179 °C for two hours, uncovering it for the last half-hour. Turn the hearts over after one hour's cooking. When ready carve into thin slices and place on a warm dish, taste the sauce for seasoning, boil for a few minutes to reduce and strengthen, then pour it over the sliced hearts. Serve with a dish of mushrooms and sauté potatoes.

For a simple Lenten dish I can't think of anything much more delicious, though hardly non-fattening, than spaghetti mixed with courgettes or, as the Italians would have it:

———— Spaghetti con zucchine ————

$1\frac{1}{2}$ lbs of spaghetti	1 stick of celery
2 lbs of zucchine	4 oz of butter, 1 tablespoon olive oil
2 shallots	1 tin (14 oz) chopped tomatoes
1 medium onion	freshly grated parmesan cheese
1 carrot	black pepper, frying oil

Try to obtain 'Filli de Cecco' spaghetti, it is in a blue cellophane packet with a jolly lady on the front.

Chop all the vegetables finely except the zucchine. Put them in a large saucepan (big enough to contain the cooked spaghetti eventually) with the butter and olive oil, cook gently until soft, add the tomatoes, season with salt and pepper, cover and simmer for half an hour. Cut the zucchine into discs of $\frac{1}{8}$ inch thick and deep fry until golden, remove from the oil with a slotted spoon and leave to drain on kitchen paper. Sprinkle them with some nice salt, keep warm. Meanwhile you have been cooking the spaghetti in the usual manner in lots of salted boiling water; drain them when they are still very much *al dente* and fling them

49

into the saucepan containing the sauce. Mix well together, cover and leave on a tiny heat to complete the cooking for about five minutes. Pour onto a great warmed dish and cover with the fried zucchine. This is ample for six fasters.

1 February 1986

Sweet somethings

'They are destined to be lost. They make foods into their God and they are proudest of something they should think shameful.' Words from last Sunday's epistle. Wow! that's telling us. Foodies beware. The only comfort is that it was written by St Paul, that notorious old grouch. That being said let's get on with the business.

I had some cream and mushrooms going bad in the refrigerator and also some of those disgusting-looking packets of frozen New Zealand lambs' sweetbreads found in Sainsbury's which are incredibly cheap. I had never tried them so I did and the results according to the uncle were the best he'd ever tasted. I cooked them by way of Madam Grigson's account of Mr Woodhouse's dish in *Emma* though those would have been lovely fresh calves' sweetbreads, which now cost a fortune if you can find them.

———— Fricassée of sweetbreads ————

4 packs of frozen sweetbreads (about 2 lbs)
1 medium onion
2 cloves of garlic
8 oz button mushrooms
2 oz butter

2 heaped desert spoons of plain flour
18 fl oz of good chicken or veal stock
10 oz of cream (half can be sour)
juice and grated peel of one lemon
salt, pepper and nutmeg

Soak the sweetbreads in cold water until thawed, then change the water, salt it and leave them to soak for an hour or two. Drain, put in a saucepan, just cover with cold water and the juice of a lemon, bring gently to the boil and simmer for five minutes. Drain again and plunge into cold water. They now look more terrible than ever; but do not despair, continue with a brave heart. Remove any obvious hard gristly skin (there wasn't much; they must very kindly have done it in New Zealand.) Place the sweetbreads between two plates with a weight on top and chill in the refrigerator. This can all be done the day before if you like. Now chop the onion and garlic quite finely and sauté gently until soft, add the little mushrooms whole, stirring them into the onions for a minute; sprinkle in the flour, cook until thoroughly amalgamated with the rest then slowly add the warmed stock and let it simmer for 15 minutes; season with ground pepper, salt, nutmeg and the grated lemon peel; pour in the cream, mix well. Now add the sweetbreads and continue simmering for another half-hour, giving the odd stir every now and then. Serve with plain rice and *petits pois* or french beans.

I thought you might like a festive pudding for Easter instead of simnel cake. This is a cheese cake made for a dear friend, Martin Harris, years ago. He is a good Jewish boy and this is nothing like his mother used to make.

─────── *Martin Harris pudding* ───────

6 digestive biscuits
8 ginger nuts
4 oz of unsalted butter
1 tablespoon of demerara sugar
1 lb of curd cheese

12 oz of caster sugar
3 large eggs
2 teaspoons of vanilla essence (not flavouring)
1 pint of soured cream

You need a baking tin with a detachable bottom measuring $9\frac{1}{2}''$ across and 2" in height. Oil it lightly. Crush the biscuits in a plastic bag with a rolling pin or some such suitable device until reduced to crumbs. Melt the butter in a saucepan, stir in the crumbs, mixing well, add the demerara sugar. Press into the base of the tin evenly with the aid of a jam-jar. Beat the curd cheese and four ounces of the sugar together, then still beating add the eggs one at a time and finally one teaspoon of the vanilla essence. Pour into the biscuit base and bake in the middle of a preheated oven at Gas 5, 375 °F, 190 °C, for 20 minutes. Remove to cool for half an hour. Mix the soured cream, two ounces of sugar and the other teaspoon of vanilla essence in a bowl and pour on top of the cooled cheese cake. Turn the oven up to Gas 6, 400 °F, 200 °C, and bake for a further ten minutes. Remove, cool, then refrigerate for a good six hours. When thoroughly chilled scatter the remaining six ounces of sugar evenly over the top. Preheat the grill for about five minutes, then place the pudding underneath. Watch it like a hawk and keep turning until you achieve a beautiful tortoiseshell brûlé. To make it truly paschal you could decorate with those ravishing tiny little sugared eggs found on the simnel cakes. When the brûlé has cooled remove the cheese cake carefully from the tin and serve with a flourish. If you happen to have one of those tins hinged at the side as well as having a detachable bottom, so much the better and easier.

1 March 1986

Scottish scoff

This is a Scottish issue so we must have Scottish aliment to the fore. We all know that Scotland produces the best meat, fish, raspberries and of course whisky, they are also some of the best bakers in the world producing pastry and scones so gossamer light they float you to a glutton's heaven. The weather continuing as it does, there is no better soup than cockaleekie:

—— Cockaleekie ——

1 boiling chicken	2½ quarts of beef or veal stock
8 leeks	bouquet garni of parsley and thyme
3 oz of butter	salt, pepper and soft brown sugar

Cut the leeks into one-inch pieces discarding the tough green part; wash very carefully under a fierce tap to remove all that clinging grit.

Joint the fowl and season lightly with ground pepper and salt. Heat the butter in a large saucepan, add the jointed fowl and the carcase, brown all over. Put in the leeks and fry for a further five minutes stirring and turning the ingredients. Pour in the stock and put in the bouquet garni wrapped in a muslin bag. Bring to the boil and skim if necessary, then simmer for two hours with the lid on. Remove chicken pieces and carcase, also the bouquet. Cut the flesh off the bones and return to the soup. Taste for seasoning adding a little brown sugar if you like. Some people add rice to this soup, which is a mistake; leave it pure. The addition of prunes is also unwise and was even severely criticised by Talleyrand. As you can see it is a meal in itself and all the better for making 24 hours ahead to be reheated when needed.

The revolting object to be found in pubs and supermarkets masquerading as a scotch egg is a veritable disgrace to its true self. Rock hard, chilled greenish eggs swathed in gristly sausage meat coated with orange gravel. Dear oh dear. The real thing is delicious, an excellent little luncheon dish served with a salad and a glass of wine.

------- *Scotch eggs* -------

10 large eggs
8 oz of ham
6 anchovy fillets

4 oz fresh breadcrumbs
black pepper and mixed spice
bacon fat or butter

Beat two eggs in shallow bowl. Put the rest of the eggs in a saucepan, cover with cold water, bring to the boil and simmer for five minutes. Plunge into cold water and peel. This method makes the yolks slightly softer, which to my mind is far more delectable.

Mince or chop finely the ham and the anchovies, combine with the breadcrumbs, ground pepper and half a teaspoon of mixed spice and the beaten eggs leaving a little of the egg mixture in the bowl. Smear each boiled egg with the remaining raw egg and encase with the ham mixture, moulding it round in your squeaky-clean hands. Fry in the bacon fat or butter with a slug of olive oil added until browned all over, cut in half and serve on fried bread or toast, calories permitting.

To return to the sweet tooth, here is a fake sort of Athole brose ice-cream covered in crumbled flapjack instead of praline. First make

Scottish flapjack

4 oz flaked oats
3 oz soft brown sugar
3 oz unsalted butter

1 dessertspoonful of golden syrup
$\frac{1}{2}$ teaspoonful of ground ginger

Blend together the butter and sugar until creamy, work in the oats and the treacle, finally sprinkle in the ginger and mix well. Turn the mixture into an eight-inch sandwich tin or pour onto a baking sheet; either one should be well greased. Flatten the mixture evenly and bake in a pre-heated oven at Gas 5, 375 °F, 190 °C, for 18 minutes. When cold remove from the tin and crumble in a plastic bag rolling and banging with a rolling pin. Store in a jar. Children make this very well so if you have any start them off.

Athole brose ice-cream

1 pint thick cream
4 level tablespoons of clear heather
  honey
6 level tablespoons of scotch whisky

Dissolve the honey in the whisky by warming it slightly in a small saucepan. When cool fold into the cream and whip all together until thick. Freeze until needed but let it soften for a while before serving. Strew the crumbled flapjack over the ice cream.

26 April 1986

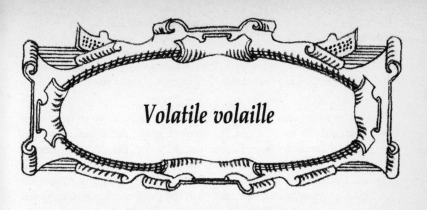

Volatile volaille

Whitsun today but as they who know better have moved the Whit Monday Bank Holiday away from Whitmonday you will be reading this just in time for the official spurious one; they should have learnt their lesson from the disastrous Mayday jollities. However, what will happen during this coming week is that the turkey breeders will be trying to make everyone get a turkey. They seem to make a splurge with the advertisements every Bank Holiday despite the obdurate British feeling that turkeys are for Christmas. They are progressing slowly, so if you happen to succumb to the idea (they are fairly cheap and children do like them; they also feed a lot of people) here is a very delicious way of brightening the leftovers after you have had the first traditional whack.

──────── Volaille de Salpicon Senegalaise ────────

For the sauce:

2 oz butter
1 tablespoon curry paste
2 tablespoons plain flour
1 to 1½ pints of the turkey stock

1 onion, finely chopped
¼ pint thick cream
handful of parsley, chopped

Melt the butter in a heavy saucepan. Stir in the curry paste and the chopped onion, cook gently for about ten minutes until soft. Add the flour, mixing thoroughly for a minute, then gradually pour in the heated stock a little at a time, until you have the required consistency of a coating sauce. Simmer for at least 20 minutes then add the cream spoonful by spoonful. Season with ground black pepper, salt and the chopped parsley. Cover and keep at the ready. Now for the rest:

2 oz butter
4 shallots finely chopped
the remains of the turkey
(say 12–16 oz)
ham or tongue (half as much as the
turkey)

4 oz dry vermouth
salt, pepper, oregano
2 hardboiled eggs
$\frac{1}{2}$ lb button mushrooms, briefly sautéd
$\frac{1}{2}$ lb cooked petits pois

Melt the butter in a frying pan or container large enough to receive the meats and the sauce. Cook the shallots gently for a minute, mix in the turkey, ham or tongue, having diced the lot. Season with ground pepper, salt and oregano then keep turning over and over until well warmed through. Pour in the vermouth, raise the heat and cook until the liquid has mostly evaporated. Stir in the peas, mushrooms, chopped boiled eggs and enough of the sauce to envelope the mixture, check the seasoning, serve with rice or noodles. You can pour it all into a fireproof dish, sprinkle with parmesan or gruyère or both and reheat in the oven at a later date.

--------- *Burnt onion and carrot rice* ---------

1 large onion
2 large carrots
8 oz long grain rice

16 fluid oz of good chicken stock
1 oz butter
2 tablespoons of olive oil

Chop the peeled onion and carrots fairly small and melt the oil and butter in a saucepan with a good tight fitting lid. Add the vegetables and cook until rather burnt, starting gently with the lid on. When charred round the edges stir in the rice until thoroughly covered with the oils, pour in the heated chicken stock, taste for seasoning. Bring to the boil giving the odd stir, cover with the lid, turn the heat as low as possible and simmer for 20 minutes, when it should be perfectly cooked and have an interesting colour. If there is still too much liquid just leave the lid off for a further five minutes tossing it about a bit. This is a good accompaniment to any well flavoured dish, or may be eaten with sprinkled parmesan for a first course.

24 May 1986

Hold the mayo

There are a lot of very terrible food advertisements that appear regularly on our television screens with ghastly plates of something with the neat piles of bright cylindrical carrots and emerald peas stuck to attention, but the worst ones are for the yellowish goo they pour out of bottles to desecrate salads and tomatoes. There is also usually some poor old egg brought into the action. Why in all the world do the British like this vile-tasting stuff called salad cream or even worse mayonnaise? It has nothing to do with either, more like a mixture of malt vinegar and Scotts Emulsion. I have even had it served with excellent salmon in an otherwise perfectly respectable country hotel in Cumberland.

Then there is the terrible question of trying to get a plain, well-dressed salad, almost impossible; along comes a limp lettuce with beetroot bleeding all over it, liberally laced with malt vinegar and strewn with the ubiquitous mustard and cress we used to grow on flannels, and some chunks of tomato thrown in for good measure — disastrous mess. Salads should remain simple and green when lettuce is used. There are of course hundreds of different salads and, now that summer has actually deigned to make an appearance, here are a few to try out.

First of all make a good dressing. Everyone has their own ideas on this most important of additions, this is mine. Get a jam jar with a well fitting top. Bruise a skinned clove of garlic, put it in the jar. Add a heaped teaspoon of salt, caster sugar, dry mustard and made up Dijon mustard, moisten with a desert spoon of lemon juice and one of red wine vinegar. A tablespoon of sherry or port makes a good flavour if you have some lying around. Grind some black pepper into the jar then stir it all together. Pour good olive oil into the mixture up to the shoulder of the jar, screw the top on, shake vigorously every time you need it. See what you think of it then add or deplete to your own taste. Most folk seem to like it.

Potato salad made from the new Jersey potatoes is one of the great dishes of the world, I think, but not that horrible stuff bought in delicatessens covered in white slime. Simply boil the potatoes in their skins. Have ready a bowl with enough dressing to anoint the amount of potatoes you have cooked. Peel the potatoes while still hot, plopping them into the dressing to coat thoroughly as soon as possible. If you want to cut them, wait until they cool or they tend to crumble. Now the all-important part; have a great bunch of parsley, chives and tarragon chopped fine, slice enough spring onions to suit your fancy (my fancy is a lot but I realise they do not suit everyone), mix carefully with the potatoes, add more oil if necessary, grind more pepper over the top and serve at will. It should have enough herbs to appear quite green.

Broad beans, young, tender and delectable are my favourite vegetable of all. Served with butter and chopped parsley they beat asparagus but they also make a heavenly salad. Boil the beans in salted water until just tender. Crush a garlic clove or two in the bottom of a bowl, add ten anchovy fillets chopped roughly. Drain the beans, mix with the anchovy mess, pour enough olive oil to dress the beans liberally, a good squeeze of lemon juice, ground black pepper and sprinkle with chopped parsley. This amount of anchovies would do for about two pounds of beans.

A good rice salad is a useful adjunct, very suitable for cold chicken dishes, but it must be well dressed and interesting. My heart always sinks at the sight of cold boiled rice mixed with sweet corn and maybe strips of raw unskinned red pepper (for the colour you know); that's it, no flavouring, no herbs, no use. Why corn anyway? Corn needs butter. This is a goodly mixture: have ready a peeled, de-seeded, cubed cucumber slightly salted, four very thinly sliced shallots, 18 stoned black olives, three sticks of celery chopped and some sliced tomatoes salted and peppered. Boil 12 oz of the rice of your choice in lots of salted boiling water with half a lemon in it. (Keep it *al dente*.) When ready, drain the rice well, place in a large bowl, salt, season and toss with about six tablespoons of olive oil, a dessert spoon of white wine vinegar, the chopped shallots and a lot of freshly grated nutmeg. Stir in all the prepared vegetables except the tomatoes, lie these on top of the rice like a blanket and strew with chopped parsley and torn basil leaves.

Finally a rather curious mushroom salad which I once concocted in despair for someone's birthday buffet. Slice a pound of button mushrooms very finely, this is done in a trice with a food processor, otherwise use a good sharp knife and patience, but they must be fine. Make a mixture of ten tablespoons of olive oil, the juice of a lemon, two tablespoons of soy sauce, four crushed cloves of garlic and a few shots of tabasco. Marinade the mushrooms in this sauce for an hour or so then add six oz of thick cream, ground salt and pepper. Make a bed of bean sprouts on a suitable dish, then pour the mushrooms into it. Strew with a generous amount of parsley and coriander chopped well.

Endless vegetables like spinach, French beans etc, make delicious salads simply dressed with good olive oil and lemon juice, the one thing to beware of is too much vinegar. It's a killer.

21 June 1986

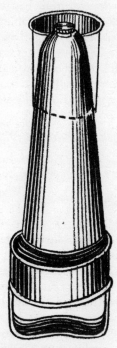

No. 23 TIN BOMB MOULD, with Screw
Very handsome.

FANCY ICE MOULDS

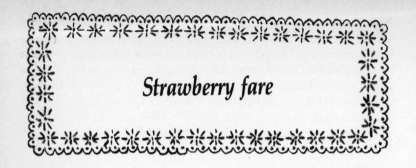

A kind firm dealing with soft fruits has sent me masses of strawberries and as our own glorious fruit are just appearing on the market I thought they could be the main theme. 'Doubtless God could have made a better berry, doubtless He never did,' nice quote from Dr Boteler in *The Compleat Angler*. Although straight strawberries and great jugs of yellow Jersey cream can hardly be bettered, the following pudding is quite something. Both rich and expensive. A party treat.

Strawberry Charlotte Malakoff

1 lb of strawberries
½ pint of cointreau or Grand Marnier
¼ pint water
½ lb best unsalted butter (softened)
¾ pint of thick cream

6 oz caster sugar
¼ teaspoon (8 drops) almond essence
6 oz fresh ground almonds
48 sponge fingers (best quality)

You need a three-pint cylindrical mould about four inches high and seven inches across, a soufflé dish would do. Line the base with a round of grease-proof paper. In a soup plate pour a quarter-pint of water and half the liqueur. Rapidly dip the sponge fingers one at a time and drain on a rack. Line the base of the mould with the fingers in a cartwheel spoke position laying them curved side down. You will have to cut them to fit snugly. Line the sides with more of the fingers with the curved sides against the mould. There should be no gaps. Cream the softened butter and sugar until pale and fluffy, beat in the rest of the liqueur and the almond essence until the sugar is totally dissolved then beat in the ground almonds. Whip the cream until it can leave a trail and fold into the almond mixture. Put a third of it in the lined mould.

Insert a layer of hulled strawberries head down, cover with a layer of sponge fingers, then repeat the operation. Fill the mould with the remaining third of almond cream and any fingers that are left as a final layer. Trim the fingers around the edge of the bowl and press them into the cream. Cover the mould with cling film or greaseproof paper, put a little plate to fit on top, and weight it with something weighing a pound or so. Refrigerate overnight. When needed run a knife round the inside of the dish and turn out onto a pretty plate. Cover with more strawberries and serve with whipped cream or a

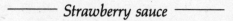

Strawberry sauce

This is an unusual sauce using green peppercorns. Melt about an ounce of butter in a saucepan, add a teaspoonful of soft green peppercorns and a pound of quartered strawberries, cook gently for two minutes carefully turning the fruit. Pour in a tablespoon of Pernod and eight ounces of Grand Marnier, let them warm, then set fire to the whole lot. When the flames die down add eight ounces of fresh orange juice. Check for sweetness. Very good with ice cream. This is recommended by the kind soft fruit firm.

Strawberry salad

For a ravishingly pretty salad peel a cucumber and slice very thinly on a mandoline. Add a little salt then place the slices between two plates with a weight on top for an hour or two returning now and then to pour liquid away. Cut an equal amount of strawberries into horizontal slices, grind some black pepper over them and sprinkle with a little wine vinegar or lemon juice. Just before you need to serve the salad arrange the two ingredients together to surround a beautiful cold fish or fowl. A delight to the eye.

Finally a plug for a nice little cook book which is being sold in aid of the Cornwall Historic Churches Trust, a very charming cause and quite a change from Ethiopia. Entitled *Men's Menus* it is just that. A collection of very different receipts from men all over Britain edited by Alice Boyd and published by the Trust. Some very good receipts they are too, including our dear Alan Watkins's efforts.

There is an hilarious introduction on the art of not cooking by Professor John Bayley, who is married to Iris Murdoch. They have some pretty weird eating habits, nothing takes more than ten minutes to prepare except vegetables, which must be soggy, and they don't clean the saucepan.

28 June 1986

Summer stock

I have been going to weddings every week this month, all those
children of what seems yesterday have turned into ravishing lasses
and strapping great lads all marching down the aisles and plighting
their troths in beautiful churches with glorious music and singing,
though what half of them make of the rows of divorced parents behind
them as they are taking their vows heaven alone knows; it must be
rather confusing. They all took place at different times and the eats
were universally excellent, adding greatly to the very joyous festivities.
Now, more food for summer occasions:

———— Chicken Veronica ————

1 4-lb boiling fowl
5 carrots, 2 onions
1 stick of celery, 1 fat clove of garlic
parsley stalks, tarragon
the rind of a lemon thinly pared

For the sauce:
$\frac{1}{2}$ pint of double cream
4 tablespoons medium sherry
4 egg yolks and $\frac{1}{4}$ pint of the stock
a little brandy or the like

I think I got this receipt from Jilly Virgin, and as she herself declared
it is extremely good. Start it the day before you need it. Rub the bird
all over with lemon juice, place in a heavy saucepan with the vegetables,
herbs and lemon peel. Just cover with water adding two tablespoons
of salt, bring to simmering point then cook very gently until tender,
about $2\frac{1}{2}$ hours. (If by chance you choose to use a roaster it will barely
need an hour but the flavour is not as good.) When ready and cooled
a bit, carve into suitably sized pieces. Remove all skin and bone, put
these all back in the stock with the giblets and cook for another three
quarters of an hour to enrich the stock for the sauce. Chill then remove
the fat.

For the sauce beat the egg yolks, the cream and the sherry together
vigorously. Bring the $\frac{1}{4}$ pint of stock to the boil and pour into the

mixture stirring with a wooden spoon. Transfer the lot into a frying pan set on a low heat and an asbestos mat; keep stirring all the time to avoid curdling until it is the consistency of cream and just coats the back of the spoon. Check the seasoning, adding ground pepper, a little lemon juice and a touch of brandy, take off the heat but continue stirring for a few minutes then pour over the chicken, leave to cool, then chill until set. Serve sprinkled with chives and tarragon and, if you like, some little seedless grapes.

I think everyone has come across the pasta salad made with the bigger pastas, tuna, etc. This one is made with spaghetti and comes from a Roman receipt, but is originally from Ischia.

Spaghetti Estivi Freddi

1½ lbs spaghetti
5 tablespoons of best olive oil
3 fat cloves of garlic chopped finely
a handful of mint or spearmint
  chopped finely

5 tablespoons of fresh orange juice
12 black olives
6 anchovy fillets
¼ lb button mushrooms preserved in
  oil

Put the oil and the garlic in a frying pan, cook gently until the garlic is golden, add the mint and take off the heat. Pour in the orange juice. Chop the olives and anchovies roughly, stir them into the pan then add the mushrooms. (You can get these mushrooms in an Italian delicatessen or marinade them yourself overnight.) Season all with salt and mix together. Cook the spaghetti in plenty of boiling salted water keeping them slightly more *al dente* than usual, drain and pour onto a wide charger, mix in the sauce and spread the spaghetti all over the charger to cool. When cold transfer to a nice rustic dish. Enough for six hearty eaters.

Here is a delicious and strange cake:

Walnut and coffee cake

4 eggs
6 oz walnuts coarsely chopped
4 oz icing sugar

1 tablespoon cocoa
1 tablespoon finely ground coffee
1 tablespoon fine fresh breadcrumbs

Separate yolks from whites. Cream yolks and sugar. Add breadcrumbs, coffee, cocoa and walnuts, mix well. Fold in the whites of egg beaten stiff. Have ready a greased and lined cake tin 8 inches in diameter, 2 inches high. Pour in mixture, bake in a preheated oven Gas 4, 350 °F, 177 °C for 45 minutes. Cool and turn out onto a rack. When cold ice with $\frac{1}{4}$ lb unsalted butter creamed with $\frac{1}{4}$ lb icing sugar and one egg yolk. Add a heaped tablespoon of instant coffee dissolved in two tablespoons of boiling water. Mix well and spread over the cake. So good!

26 July 1986

Farce food

The poor old vegetable marrow always seems to get a very bad press, especially in childhood memories. The terrible vision of over-cooked green slime lying in a pool of water, coated with wallpaper paste, lingers. I am very fond of the old dear and find its taste and texture rather comforting just so long as it never gets near water. Fried in olive oil with a little garlic or steamed with some tarragon it makes a very good accompaniment to any strong or dry dish. There are lots of the small marrows in the market at present, so try this stuffed version. Never get large ones; they get very tough and tasteless. Nine to twelve inches is big enough.

———— *Stuffed vegetable marrow* ————

2 small marrows
8oz best sausage meat
8oz minced beef
8oz minced pork/lamb/veal
1 lb streaky bacon rashers
5 anchovy fillets in oil
3 fat cloves of garlic

3 medium onions
3 medium carrots
parsley, sage, thyme, allspice
the thin peel of a lemon, grated
1 tablespoon tomato purée, olive oil
tabasco and Worcester sauce
1 large egg, salt and pepper

Peel the marrows, cut in half longways, scoop out the seeds and pith. Sprinkle with salt. Chop all the vegetables, garlic and anchovies very fine, add a bunch of chopped parsley, a good pinch of thyme and sage and $\frac{1}{4}$ teaspoon of allspice and the lemon peel. Mix into the minced meats and sausage. Season with ground salt and pepper, a generous dash of tabasco and Worcester sauce, break in the egg and a tablespoon or so of olive oil, then mix all together very thoroughly. Stuff the cavities of the marrows with the mixture and close them. Place in a baking dish. Lay the rashers of bacon to encircle the marrows, tucking the ends under, sprinkle with rosemary and a drizzle of olive oil. Bake in a preheated oven at Gas 2, 310 °F, 150 °C for three hours. Plenty for eight to ten folk. It is very good cold, cut into thick slices. Serve with a fresh tomato sauce.

For the following receipt, the best way to purchase the mushrooms is to go to a supermarket with a nice little box and pick out the biggest and most uniform ones from the loose array. Reckon on four mushrooms per person.

——— *Stuffed mushrooms* ———

24 large button mushrooms
2 oz minced onion
2 fat cloves of garlic
2 tablespoons chopped parsley
2 oz fine, fresh breadcrumbs

4 oz chopped smoked ham or bacon
4 oz freshly grated parmesan/gruyère
good stock and seasoning
olive oil

Pluck out the mushroom stalks and chop. Crush the garlic and fry gently in two tablespoons of olive oil with the stalks and onion until soft but not browned. Stir in the parsley, breadcrumbs, cheese and ham, season with ground salt and pepper. Moisten with enough stock to the consistency of a porridge. Spoon this mixture into the mushroom caps. Oil a large dish or baking tray and place the mushrooms on it (you may need two trays). Sprinkle with olive oil. Bake in a preheated oven at Gas 5, 380 °F, 193 °C, for 20 minutes. Serve as a vegetable or as a first course with triangles of toast or fried bread.

Here is a Hungarian stuffed vegetable receipt, useful for using up leftover meats.

——— *Stuffed green pepper salad* ———

6 large green capsicum peppers
4 fluid oz white wine vinegar
1 lb roast veal/pork/chicken or
   whatever, chopped
2 hard-boiled eggs, chopped
2 medium potatoes, boiled and sieved

2 pickled cucumbers, peeled and
   chopped fine
12 oz mayonnaise
12 thick tomato slices
1 envelope of gelatine
11 fluid oz hot chicken stock

Bake the peppers in a preheated oven at Gas 2, 310 °F, 154 °C, just long enough so you can peel them with ease without any breaks. Cut in half crossways, remove pith and seeds. Make a marinade of the vinegar, 4 oz water, salt and pepper, soak the peppers in it for an hour. Mix the meat, eggs, potatoes, pickle and mayonnaise together, fill the peppers and put a slice of tomato on each. Soften the gelatine in 2 oz cold water, then dissolve in hot stock. Let it cool until syrupy. Brush the peppers with the stock, chill for 15 minutes, repeat, then put them on a pretty dish in the refrigerator. Let the rest of the gelatine set, cut into dice and sprinkle around the peppers.

23 August 1986

25

a

H A R E

Bismarck Rhubarb

Duchess of York Mousses
Petites Mousses à la Duchesse de York

Princess May Chicken Soufflés
Petits Soufflés de Volailles à la Princesse May

Vieille cuisine

I noticed in the *Times* a couple of weeks ago an article by Shona Crawford Poole (such a lovely name). She was having a terrible time trying to find a properly poached egg. Hers were served tasting of various vinegars, as it is meant to coagulate the white of the egg, but that has always been a disgusting idea and I feel for her dismay. The various other methods were very complicated, so I shall tell you the secret of the perfect poached egg, neatly formed with no whirling tentacles. James Coats, a great travelling friend of mine, discovered this method in a ship crossing the Atlantic.

Bring a frying pan of salted water to simmering point. Place an excellent egg in its shell into the water then roll it round and round whilst intoning two Our Fathers and one Hail Mary: about half a minute. Remove egg from the water with a perforated spoon, then break into the just trembling water, cover with a lid and cook for as long as you fancy. Drain well in the spoon and serve as desired. The rolling of the egg in hot water will have set the white a tiny bit so when you crack it, it retains a nice shape.

Another old-fashioned favourite of mine which is hard to find nowadays is soft herring roes on toast. They are absolutely delicious, very cheap and I'm sure frightfully good for you if you are into health.

———— Herring roes on toast ————

soft herring roes
lemons
plain flour
cayenne pepper, salt

thin streaky unsmoked bacon
parsley, chopped
butter and sunflower oil

Get fine fresh plump roes, about four per person. Wash under running hot water; this will remove the slime and stiffen them up. Drain on paper kitchen towels. Put enough flour in a plastic bag, then gently shake the roes in it to coat all over. Remove from the bag, shake off surplus flour and lay on some greaseproof paper. Melt the butter with a slurp of oil in a good heavy frying pan; when it is just sizzling put in the roes and cook gently until golden brown on both sides. If you are dealing with more than one panful keep the cooked roes warm in the oven having removed them from the pan and drained them on some kitchen towel. Grill the bacon until brittle. Have ready some hot toast spread with anchovy paste or Gentleman's Relish. Pile the roes onto the toasts, sprinkle with cayenne pepper and a touch of salt, crumble the bacon over the top and strew with chopped parsley. Serve with wedges of lemon.

I have just returned from my annual visit to Cockermouth, Cumberland, whence I brought you a marvellous coffee pudding last year, the concoction of my host Patricius Senhouse. Here is his first-class and simple receipt to make chutney.

———— Patricius's pickle ————

3 lbs cooking apples, peeled, cored
  and chopped
1 lb soft brown sugar
1 lb stoneless raisins
1 lb stoneless dates
2 lbs onions chopped

1 quart of white malt vinegar
1 dessert spoonful of rock salt
1 teaspoon of cayenne pepper
$\frac{1}{4}$ oz each of cloves, cinnamon,
  peppercorns

Tie the cloves and peppercorns in a scrap of muslin attached to a string so you can remove them later. Put all the ingredients into a large saucepan. Bring to the boil and simmer until the required consistency is achieved, taking care to leave plenty of liquid or it will dry out later in the jar. Leave to cool, then put into good screwtop jars, having discarded the muslin bag with its contents. Particularly good with cold pork or lamb.

I am constantly amazed but bewildered by the extraordinary fruit and curious vegetables that appear in the super- and ordinary markets today. The usual response to my inquiries as to what to do with them is 'Treat them like potatoes,' which I'm sure is, if not wrong, inadequate. Help is now to hand. There is a wonderful new Jane Grigson book, *Exotic Fruits and Vegetables* (Jonathan Cape). Not only does it inform and give various ideas and receipts but is really beautifully illustrated by Charlotte Knox with 19th-century-style coloured drawings of every fruit and vegetable described. A joy to behold. There is a very sinister bunch of roots called *Boesenbergia pandurata* or Chinese key which is for fish curries or for soothing elephants' muscles and joints. Obviously an irresistible 'must' for all.

20 September 1986

Rustication

We are immensely fortunate in Victoria to have not only a first class market and an excellent fishmonger but also one of the best Italian delicatessens in London, Gastronomia Italia, and they are all in Tachbrook Street, Upper and Lower. The delicatessen is run by Mario Diannunzio (what a name to conjure with) a splendid Glaswegian Italian with large moustachios. They have the most exciting salamis and sausages from all over Italy and produce daily, fresh pizzas at lunch time. There is always a queue; but the thing I find irresistible is a huge cake-shaped bread they make called *rustica* full of delicious morsels of the different meats and made from the pizza dough. This is how they make it, as far as I can gather.

—— *Rustica bread* ——

1 lb plain flour
1 level teaspoon of salt
$\frac{1}{2}$ oz fresh yeast
$\frac{1}{2}$ pint tepid water
2 tablespoons olive oil

1 egg
6 oz chopped mixed meats, (salami, mortadella, prosciutto ham etc.)
black pepper
a few black olives, stoned.

Blend the yeast with the water, add the oil. Mix into the flour until you have a pliable dough which leaves the sides of the bowl. Turn out onto a floured board and knead and stretch for about seven minutes or do the whole thing in a food processor in a moment. Make it into a ball and leave in an oiled bowl, covered, in a warm place until it has doubled its size. When it has risen turn out onto a board and lightly knead the chopped meats, the beaten egg, ground pepper and salt into it, including any chopped ham fat. Place in an oiled cake tin, brush the top with a little beaten white of egg and bake in a preheated oven at Gas 4, 400 °F, 179 °C, for about an hour. Raise the temperature for the last ten minutes to make a nice brown top. Turn out and let cool if you can resist tearing at it while still warm. Cut in hunks.

I think the above must be a poor relation to the *pizza rustica* which has nothing to do with pizzas. It is a pork and cheese pie cooked in a sweet pastry, very unusual and surprisingly good. I don't think you can better Marcella Hazan's receipt, she cuts out half the sugar and uses no cinnamon.

─────── *Pizza rustica* ───────

For the pastry:
8 oz plain flour
2 egg yolks
pinch of salt

4 oz unsalted butter cut into small
   pieces
3 tablespoons iced water
1 oz granulated sugar

Mix all the ingredients together and knead briefly by hand or in a food processor. Wrap dough in cling film and refrigerate for at least an hour.

For the filling:
2 egg yolks
12 oz whole milk ricotta cheese
8 oz roughly chopped mortadella,
   salami, ham, prosciutto (mixed)

4 oz mozzarella diced
2 tablespoons fresh grated parmesan
salt and black pepper

Beat the eggs and ricotta in a bowl until creamy. Add the chopped meats, mozzarella, parmesan. Season liberally with salt and freshly ground pepper. Butter a two-pint soufflé dish or similar object. Cut off a third of the dough and roll it into a round on some foil large enough to line the bottom of the dish and come a little way up the sides. Turn the dough into the dish, peel away the foil. Take another third of the dough, roll into strips the height of the bowl (on foil again) and line the sides of the bowl, pressing and overlapping when necessary. Pour the mixture from the other bowl into the pastry case, press lightly to force out any air bubbles. Roll out the remaining dough into a circle to make a generous lid for the pie (on foil again). Place on top of pie, peel away foil, press edges tightly against lining to form a tight seal and trim off neatly. Smooth all rough connections with a wet finger. Bake in the upper level of a preheated oven Gas 5, 375 °F, 190 °C, for 45 minutes. Turn up the heat for an extra five minutes to brown.

18 October 1986

Cod and cake

Advent is lurking round the corner and Christmas Eve is getting depressingly near, egged on by those in Oxford Street with their premature caverns for the kiddies and dolled up Santa Clauses at the ready to extort and blackmail the bewildered parents into vast spending sprees for dangerous toys and sickening little dolls. So I return with pleasure to my beloved salt cod which I consider a suitable and delicious dish in all its forms for both fasting and feasting.

This is another receipt from my fond and faithful friend John Cobb in Cacilhas, Portugal.

——— [Bolinhos de bacalhau] (Salt codfish balls) ———

1 lb salt cod	liqueur glass of port or madeira or
¾ lb floury potatoes	sherry
1 largish onion	salt, pepper and nutmeg
8 eggs	parsley

Soak the salt cod as usual for 24 to 36 hours in plenty of cold water with frequent changes of the water. Cook the potatoes in their skins, peel them then purée through a mouli. Boil the soaked fish until tender (about 20 to 25 minutes). Drain well, remove all skin and bones. Place the flaked fish in a stout cloth and rub it until it is well shredded. Chop the onion and a good bunch of parsley finely. Put the fish, onion, parsley, and puréed potatoes into a large mixing bowl, pour in the wine, beat all together and season with fresh ground black pepper and salt. Break in the eggs one by one until the correct consistency is achieved to form little fish balls, not too sloppy. You may need only seven eggs, depending on their size and the quality of the potatoes. Using two soup spoons, shape the *bolinhos* into smallish oval fish cakes. Deep-fry in oil until really golden and crispy on the outside. Garnish with parsley and serve with plain boiled rice and a tomato salad. They also can be used as canapés with drinks where they make a welcome and excellent change.

'When really well made, even the true Portuguese Brit, normally shuddering at the thought of bacalhau, never hesitates to make a complete beast of him or herself.' Another receipt for this fish is a sort of piperade with no peppers, I love it.

─────── *Bacalhau à bras* ───────

1 lb salt cod	6 eggs
1 lb potatoes	3 tablespoons olive oil
3 medium onions	sunflower oil
1 fat clove of garlic	black olives and parsley

Prepare the fish in the usual way, soaking, boiling and shredding as above. Peel the potatoes then cut into very fine strips with the use of a mandoline or food processor if you have them, otherwise your own good knife. Chop the onions and garlic finely. Put enough sunflower oil into a frying pan to cook the potatoes. Sauté until just turning golden. Meanwhile, in another pan, simmer the onions and garlic in the olive oil until they become transparent, stir in the fish until it is thoroughly impregnated with the oil. Beat the eggs lightly, season with a fair amount of salt and ground black pepper. Scoop the potatoes out of their pan with a perforated weapon and add to the fish mixture; pour the beaten eggs in, stirring over a gentle heat until they become creamy. Serve at once scattered with a generous amount of black olives and chopped parsley. This is a very good supper dish and would do for about four hearty eaters. Green salad and red wine is all it needs.

Now for feasting here is dark and dangerous

Chocolate cake

5 oz of self-raising flour
1 oz of cocoa powder
6 oz of butter
6 oz of soft brown sugar
4 oz plain chocolate (Menier)

4 large eggs
1 teaspoon of vanilla essence
For the icing:
½ lb chocolate (Menier)
2 egg yolks

Cream together the butter, sugar, vanilla and the chocolate melted in 3 tablespoons of boiling water. Separate the eggs. Add the yolks one by one beating sturdily. Sieve the flour and cocoa, fold into the mixture. Whip the egg whites stiffly, fold them in lightly. Spoon fairly into two 8″ cake tins that have been well buttered. Cook in the centre of a preheated oven at Gas 4, 355° F, 179° C for 25 to 30 minutes. Turn out on racks to cool. For the icing, melt the chocolate in 3 tablespoons of strong coffee, add egg yolks one at a time beating until thick. Put half in the middle of the cake and half on top.

15 November 1986

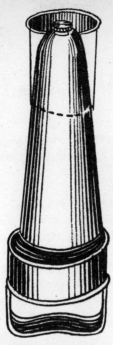

No. 23 TIN BOMB MOULD, with Screw
Very handsome.

FANCY ICE MOULDS

12½ inches long 13s 6d each
No. 30 - CUCUMBER.

8¼ inches long 2s 6d each
No. 31 — ASPARAGUS

A right royal luncheon

Guess what. Last week we had the honour of having His Royal Highness the Prince of Wales to luncheon here. What an excitement! We had sniffer dogs, sniffer detectives, idiot traffic wardens who tried to stop me bringing the food in and new table napkins. What next? H.R.H. was nice as could be, visited me twice in the kitchen where I got it all wrong and called him your majesty in mid-curtsy (dear, oh dear), but otherwise I think all went well. I thought I would tell you what the menu was, as it occurred to me that it would make an ideal alternative Christmas lunch.

First of all we had *cevice* for which I wanted halibut but had not realised that it was practically unobtainable. However my splendid fishmonger John Wright, of the elegant boater, on Warwick Way, Victoria, summoned Neptune during the night and produced the most wonderful piece of fish I have ever seen. Cost a king's ransom, which seemed appropriate. This receipt is from David Queensberry, one of the best cooks in London, and is simple, direct and totally delicious.

——— Halibut cevice ———

halibut (or any firm white fish, monk etc)
limes or lemons
onion

freshly ground salt and pepper
the best olive oil
chopped parsley

Skin and fillet the fish, then cut into strips about 3 ins × 1 in and $\frac{1}{4}$ in thick. Cut the onion into thickish rings. Place both in an upright container which has a tight-fitting lid. Season with some sea salt and enough lime juice to cover the fish. Mix well together, cover and leave in the refrigerator for twelve hours turning and shaking it every now and then. In this manner the lime juice will 'cook' the fish. Before serving squeeze the juice from the fish and remove the pieces of onion. Arrange the strips of fish in some elegant dish, dribble first class olive oil all over, season with ground black pepper and more salt if necessary. Sprinkle with finely chopped parsley. Eat with good bread or toast.

For the second course I plumped for guinea-fowl, feeling it to be not too controversial; if you know they are reared in torture chambers please do not advise. I based this receipt on Teresa Waugh's method from the *Entertaining Book* with a few additions. It is enough for eight.

--------- *Roast guinea-fowl* ---------

2 guinea-fowl
$\frac{1}{2}$ lb best sausage meat
$\frac{1}{2}$ lb chicken livers
4 ozs fresh breadcrumbs
salt, pepper
pinch of thyme

2 tablespoons of brandy
5 ozs vermouth – Chambéry
streaky bacon – unsmoked
1 beaten egg
carrots, onions, celery
chicken stock, butter

Butter an oven dish liberally. Chop enough carrots, onions and celery as fine as possible to make a good bed on the base. Put in a pre-heated oven, Gas 4, 355° F, 179° C, covered in foil while you stuff the birds. Chop the chicken livers and an onion, mix with the sausage meat and the breadcrumbs, season and add the thyme. Brown rapidly in frying pan with 2 ozs of butter. Remove from heat then beat in the egg and brandy. Stuff the birds with this mixture. Loosen the skin over the breasts and insert strips of the bacon, as much as you can fit. Butter the birds and place on the bed of vegetables that have been cooking. Put the piece of foil over them, raise the oven to Gas 5, 380° F, 190° C. Cook for half an hour. Remove the foil, douse with the vermouth and pour some chicken stock into the vegetables. Return to the oven to cook for another half hour. When ready place the birds on a dish, carve and pour the juice from the vegetables all over the meat. We had rice and little French beans to accompany this, together with the braised vegetables. Cooked in this manner the birds are not at all dry (which seems to be their besetting sin) and they have a very good flavour.

I hope you all have a splendid Christmas. You can invent your own puddings. We just had magnificent cheeses and fruit.

20/27 December 1986

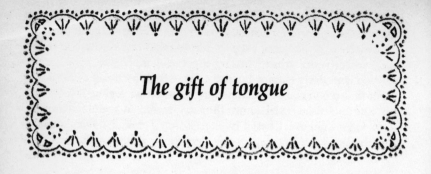

The gift of tongue

I can never understand why sliced cold tongue is so expensive to buy in shops. Bought raw it is incredibly good value with very little waste. You just boil it, skin it, coil it into a round dish, weight it for a few hours, turn it out and it is covered in lovely jelly, looks terribly professional and costs about a quarter of the shop price. I think the British are a bit squeamish about tongue presented in any other way but on a cold platter or in a sandwich. You rarely find it on a menu or in other people's houses, which is crazy, as an average ox tongue will feed from six to eight, is quite delicious and can be served in many different ways, as is only too obvious once you cross the Channel. This is my most favourite method I think. Do take the plunge: try one.

——— Braised ox tongue in madeira sauce ———

an ox tongue
For the sauce:
2 oz butter
½ lb each of carrots, onions and celery
4 oz of chopped ham
1 pint of good beef stock

1 dessertspoon of tomato purée
a bay leaf and a good pinch of thyme
2 dessertspoons of cornflour
4 oz dry madeira
salt and pepper

You can get excellent, ready-prepared tongues in Sainsburys with instructions for time of boiling. Otherwise ask your butcher to trim one for you. Place in a large heavy saucepan, cover with cold water and bring to just a trembling boil. If unsalted, add some salt. Cook for two hours at the tremble with the lid half on. Remove the tongue from the pan and plunge into cold water for a second. Leave it in the sink until you can handle it, then peel the skin off. Trim any fatty bits off the thick end. Carve into fairly substantial slices (about ⅜ of an inch) trying to keep them uniform. Start vertically at the thick end and then get more and more diagonal as you progress to the tip. If all the slices end up the same you are a great carver.

Now for the sauce. Dice the vegetables finely. Heat the butter in a saucepan, stir in the ham and the vegetables, cover and cook gently until tender and slightly browned. Mix in the tomato purée, the bay leaf and the thyme, pour in the stock, simmer the lot for 30 minutes. Meanwhile put the cornflour in a little bowl and slowly add the madeira until quite smooth. (If madeira is tricky use dry sherry.) Take the saucepan off the heat when ready and beat in the madeira mixture. Return to the heat, simmer for about two minutes until the sauce thickens. Season with salt and fresh ground pepper.

Arrange the sliced tongue in a suitable oven dish with a cover, pour the sauce all over the slices, cover and cook in a preheated slow oven Gas 2, 310° F, 154° C for 40 minutes, until the tongue is tender to the pierce. Serve with mashed potatoes and green peas, or my parsnip purée of November '85 goes very well with it.

Another rather under-used dish is cooked red cabbage. I hate it pickled in vinegar as I do all things pickled in vinegar. You might just as well drink vinegar alone as it removes any other taste completely. But fragrant hot red cabbage is wonderful with many winter dishes, game, hams or, as we had it at Christmas, with goose. I happened to have a bag of unwanted cranberries which I added to the cabbage. It was very successful.

——— *Spiced red cabbage* ———

one medium red cabbage
1 lb of cranberries (optional)
1 lb of cooking apples
1 lb of onions
5 oz red wine
2 oz red wine vinegar

4 tablespoons of soft brown sugar
4 cloves of garlic
$\frac{1}{4}$ teaspoon each of mace and
    cinnamon, 6 cloves
peel and juice of an orange, bay leaf
4 oz good dripping or butter

Core the cabbage and slice finely. Peel the apples, onions and garlic; chop roughly. Melt the fat in a large saucepan, stir in all these ingredients to coat with fat and cook gently for about 15 minutes to soften a bit. Peel the orange very thinly so that no pith adheres, cut into strips and add to cabbage together with its juice. Add all the herbs and spices (just pinch the clove heads into the pot or you will find those nasty little sticks stuck in your teeth), the wine, the vinegar and the sugar. Season with salt and pepper, cover and cook slowly until tender (quite a long time). When you feel it is almost ready add the cranberries for the last 15 minutes. These bright red rather bitter berries look marvellous against the bishop's purple. This amount will feed an army so halve it if you like, but it keeps well and could doubtless be frozen.

17 January 1987

Gammon and gangsters

This Saturday is Valentine's Day but poor old St Valentine has been struck off the rolls whilst the Mafiosi are still massacring everybody or having huge trials in Palermo or America. The only ones who have come out on top are the makers of cards and heart-shaped boxes. That shows somewhere somebody loves somebody else; isn't that nice? There do not appear to be any special dainties reserved for this day, just chocs and posies, so I bid it farewell and get on to a good robust dish of ham.

Leeks, apart from being one of the most delicious vegetables in any form, have a flavour which has always combined most beautifully with ham. I know they are hell to clean, but they are well worth it, and if they are going to be chopped up, cutting them into chunks for washing makes the earth drop out quite easily under a running tap.

Buy a good piece of gammon weighing at least 4 lbs. I use the unsmoked but either is fine. Soak for 12 hours, changing the water a few times. Put it in a saucepan more or less its own size and cover completely with cold water, bring to simmering point very slowly and cook at a bare tremble for half an hour to the pound from the moment you put it on to cook. Take it off the heat and leave for 20 minutes to 'rest', then turn it into the sink to peel the rind off. While all this is happening get on with the leeks and sauce.

Ham with leeks and cream sauce

the gammon as above
2 lbs leeks
3 oz of butter
3 tablespoons of plain flour
8 oz of dry vermouth

1 pint of milk
8 oz thick cream
2 oz freshly grated gruyère cheese
salt and pepper

Put the leeks through the slicing device of a food processor or slice very finely. Melt the butter in a saucepan and stew the leeks until tender. Add the flour, stirring until all is amalgamated, pour in the warmed vermouth little by little and then the warmed milk, stirring all the time. Season with a generous amount of ground black pepper but very little salt. Simmer for 20 minutes on an asbestos mat, giving the odd stir, then add the cream and the cheese. Check the seasoning, remembering that the ham will be salty.

Carve the ham into slices. Pour half the sauce into a shallow earthenware oven dish, arrange the sliced ham in one layer, then cover with the rest of the sauce. Dot with tiny bits of butter and bake in a hot oven for ten minutes. Finish off under the grill until brown and bubbly. Serve with simple boiled potatoes (there are some excellent Cypriot boilers in the market at the moment) and something bright green, such as broccoli. This is enough for eight to ten people but it is also a good way of using up leftover ham, using half the amount of leeks and sauce.

If you are feeling really tender and romantic you could make a Valentine surprise pudding by moulding some very good vanilla ice-cream into the shape of a heart and putting it in the freezer while you make cherries jubilée to serve with it. Very easy, exciting and good.

Cherries jubilée

1 lb tin of stoned cherries
grated rind of one lemon
2 oz of caster sugar
good pinch of cinnamon

3 tablespoons of kirsch or similar
1 dessertspoon of cornflour
4 oz cognac
3 tablespoons granulated sugar

Bulgaria produces some very good cherries, look out for them. Strain the fruit but reserve the juice. Mix the cherries with the lemon rind, caster sugar, cinnamon and kirsch and steep until needed. When you are about ready for the ice-cream blend the cornflour with the juices which the cherries have been steeping in until quite smooth, then add a few spoons of the tinned juice; pour into a frying pan and stir over a low heat until thickened. Pour in more cherry juice if necessary. Stir in the cherries to heat thoroughly, sprinkle with the granulated sugar, add the warmed cognac, then set fire to the whole thing, spooning the mixture up and down until the flames abate. Serve over your heart-shaped ice-cream which you have had at the ready, transferred to the refrigerator in a dainty dish. It will probably look like the Capone massacre, thus serving two purposes. Finish off with a tender kiss, having first wiped your face carefully with a napkin.

14 February 1987

In the purple

Aubergines, melanzane, what beautiful names! It is such a come-down for them to dwindle into egg plant. These gorgeous vegetables seem particularly suitable for this season, clothed as they are in their splendid lenten vestments, so I thought I would concentrate on them. First of all, when buying them always go for the plump shiny ones, the wrinkled specimens without the glossy waxy appearance are stale, and heaven knows what may lurk within. There are many receipts for aubergine salad, sometimes called poor man's caviare (and how). I made this one for the boys here the other day and nobody knew what it was, so spread the good news.

———— *Aubergine purée* ————

8 good-sized aubergines	6 dessertspoons of tomato purée
2 onions, chopped finely	1 dessertspoon of sugar
4 cloves of garlic	olive oil
1 lemon	salt and black pepper

Remove the stem and prickly green cap from the aubergines, caress each one with olive oil and place on baking trays in a preheated oven at Gas 6, 400° F, 205° C. Bake for 45 minutes until quite soft when pierced. Once cool enough to handle, cut in half and scoop out the innards. Chop or process finely. Sweat the onions in about six tablespoons of olive oil in a pan large enough to incorporate the aubergine mess. Cover onions when soft, add the mess plus the crushed garlic, tomato purée, juice and zest of the lemon, sugar, then season with salt and a quantity of fresh ground pepper. Cook uncovered, stirring now and then until the contents are nice and thick and any extraneous juices have gone. Check the seasoning, remove to a suitable dish to cool, then chill well. Serve with two tablespoons of chopped parsley stirred into it and surround with black olives and tomatoes. Have some hot toast or good crusty bread on the side.

One of the more delicious Italian methods of dealing with aubergines is a wonderful gooey, piping hot oven dish.

──── Melanzane alla parmigiana ────

6 large aubergines
8 oz mozzarella cheese, finely sliced

4 oz parmesan cheese, freshly grated
olive oil, salt and pepper, tomato sauce

Remove stem and cap from the aubergines, cut lengthways into $\frac{1}{4}''$ slices, sprinkle with salt and leave in a sieve or collander with a weight on top for an hour. Make a tomato sauce – heat a small coffee cup of oil, add two crushed garlic cloves, a 28-oz tin of plum tomatoes, four tablespoons of tomato purée, stir all together, season to taste with salt, pepper and a little sugar, cover and simmer for half an hour then mix in some basil or oregano. Keep at the ready. Pat the sliced aubergines dry then fry until golden in olive oil. Drain on paper towels or newspaper, grind pepper over them. You will have to do all this in batches but never mind. Make sure the oil is nice and hot if you need to add more (as you will) before frying another batch. Put a layer of aubergine at the bottom of a casserole, then a layer of mozzarella, a layer of tomato sauce and a sprinkle of parmesan, continue this way until everything is used up, ending with a good layer of parmesan to form a crust. Bake in a preheated oven at Gas 4, 355° F, 150° C, for 35 to 45 minutes. This is very rich and needs a green salad and robust red wine. Heaven.

Finally a pasta using aubergines.

──── Tagliatelle with sausage and aubergines ────

1 lb of really good meaty pork sausages
1 large aubergine
3 tablespoons of sunflower oil

$\frac{1}{2}$ lb of fat streaky bacon, finely chopped
$\frac{1}{4}$ lb of freshly grated parmesan cheese
18 oz tagliatelle

Put the sausages in boiling water for five minutes, remove and cut into one-inch lengths. Cut the aubergine into small dice and fry briskly in the oil for two minutes. In another pan cook the bacon gently until transparent, then add the sausages, turn up the heat and also fry briskly for a couple of minutes. Meanwhile your tagliatelle have been cooking in plenty of salted water; when ready, drain them but save a little of the water they were cooked in. Place the pasta in a heated dish, pour the sausage and bacon over it, put two tablespoons of the saved water into the used pan and scrape up any bits, add to the pasta together with the fried aubergines and grated cheese. Mix thoroughly and gently. Serve at once.

14 March 1987

12

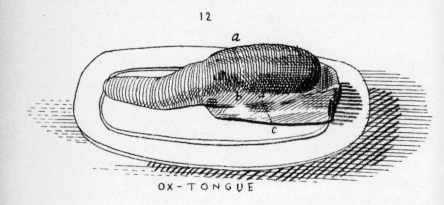

OX-TONGUE

Too many cooks

Yesterday I went to a champagne reception, no less, to celebrate the winners of the Commis Chef of the Year 1987 competition sponsored by the Académie Culinaire de France (UK). All the grand chefs were there in their whites and medals. They had been doing the judging in the afternoon and just imagine – they found the food so filthy that no one won and no prizes were given. Wasn't that a brave decision? Let's hope they all pull their aprons up for next year. We drank lovely Bollinger and munched perfectly delicious smoked salmon so all was not lost, Jack.

I was thinking how good Omelette Arnold Bennett is, but like all omelettes it is impossible to do for many people; so using the same ingredients more or less I made a mousse. It was rather good and very easy.

——— Arnold Bennett mousse ———

12 eggs
$\frac{3}{4}$ lb of smoked haddock, cooked and flaked
$\frac{1}{2}$ pt of thick cream
1 envelope of gelatine (11 g or 0.4 oz)
$\frac{1}{4}$ pt dry vermouth
2 tablespoons of freshly grated parmesan cheese
salt and pepper
1 tablespoon sunflower oil

Put the gelatine into the vermouth and leave to get spongy. Scramble ten of the eggs gently in a bowl over a saucepan of simmering water or in a bain-marie if you have one, using the oil instead of the usual butter. When they are scrambled but still creamy, stir in the gelatine and the parmesan cheese until thoroughly dissolved. Turn out into a cool bowl. Whip the cream slightly until it makes a trail, add to the eggs. Mix in the cooked haddock. Grind a generous amount of black pepper into the mousse and salt to your own requirements. Pour into a rinsed out loaf tin $9\frac{1}{4}'' \times 5\frac{1}{4}'' \times 2\frac{3}{4}''$ or some other suitable dish and chill for at least six hours. When ready to serve, run a knife round the edges and turn onto a pretty plate surrounded by tiny cherry tomatoes and black olives. Hard boil the remaining two eggs, chop and sprinkle over the top with a little parsley.

Another first course I tried recently was from a newspaper and may have been one of Fay Maschler's recipes in the *Evening Standard* some time ago; it was from a friend in Ibiza, I recall, so many thanks to whoever produced it.

———— *Courgette pâté with tomato dressing* ————

2 lbs of courgettes
3 medium onions
6 oz of fresh white breadcrumbs
3 eggs
1 tablespoon of chopped tarragon
1 tablespoon of chopped mint

1 heaped teaspoon of cornflour
salt, pepper and nutmeg
3 tablespoons of olive oil
2 lbs fresh spinach, washed, cooked
 and chopped

Slice the courgettes and the onions finely and stew in the olive oil until soft, then mash them into a pulp. Stir in the cornflour, mix well then remove from the heat; stir in the breadcrumbs, herbs, the eggs well beaten, season with salt, fresh ground pepper and nutmeg; make sure that the already cooked and chopped spinach is as drained as possible — wring it in your hands. Oil a dish or tin as in the preceding recipe, put half the courgette mixture in it, then spread the spinach over the surface adding the rest of the courgettes on top. Cover with an oiled piece of foil, place in another oven-proof container with water in it and bake in a pre-heated oven, Gas mark 2, 310° F, 154° C, for an hour. Let it cool, then chill for six hours, turn out and serve with this tomato dressing: cut four good tomatoes into small dice, sprinkle with a teaspoon of sugar, salt and a lot of ground pepper. Stir in six tablespoons of best olive oil and two of wine vinegar.

For an Easter treat you could make *petits pots au chocolat* in the blender, which takes but a trice.

———— *Petits pots au chocolat* ————

6 oz Menier chocolate
$\frac{1}{2}$ pt of single cream
4 drops of vanilla essence

pinch of salt
1 egg

Break the chocolate into a blender. Bring the cream to boiling point and pour over the chocolate. Whizz for a moment or two with the lid on. Add the egg, salt and vanilla. Whizz again until all are amalgamated.

Pour into the little pots or whatever and chill for at least 24 hours. It only gets better and denser the longer you leave it, within reason. A little freshly ground coffee sprinkled on top doesn't come amiss.

11 April 1987

In the soup

Clare Asquith my beauteous colleague the Literary Assistant had been pasting my receipts into a book and tells me I have only produced one soup, and that was Cockaleekie (which caused a lot of trouble). I thought in the brilliant days of a week ago to write about delicious cold soups for summer. But having turned the central heating on for 1 May, I feel a little downhearted about the project, tempting fate and all that. But a proper summer must come later, so I shall continue as planned.

Chicken stock is suitable for most soups and very easily made. I keep any old chicken bones in the freezer until I have a goodly collection then boil them in water with a carrot, an onion, parsley stalks and a bay leaf for an hour; strain, cool, chill, remove fat then freeze until needed.

Jerusalem artichokes with their distinctive taste make a wonderful chilled soup:

——— Iced Jerusalem soup ———

2 lbs Jerusalem artichokes
8 oz onions
4 oz medium sherry
2 pints of chicken stock

$\frac{1}{2}$ pt of thick cream
salt, pepper
chopped chives and parsley
4 oz of butter

87

Scrub the artichokes clean, no need to peel them. Slice them and the peeled onions. Melt the butter in a large saucepan, sweat the onions for ten minutes or so until softened, add the artichokes and the sherry, stir all together, cover and simmer for 20 minutes: add the stock, continue to simmer until the vegetables are soft. Season with salt and fresh ground pepper. Leave to cool a little, then liquidise the lot in a blender, a pint at a time. Chill in a suitable container until wanted. Before serving, stir in the cream thoroughly, pour into charming little bowls and strew with the chopped herbs.

———— *Iced cream of cucumber soup* ————

3 large cucumbers
2 oz of butter
3 desertspoons of plain flour
$1\frac{1}{2}$ pints of chicken stock
$\frac{1}{2}$ pint of milk

1 medium onion sliced fine
$\frac{1}{4}$ pint of thick or sour cream
salt, pepper
mint leaves

Put the onion and milk in a small saucepan, bring to the boil, remove from the heat and leave to seethe. Peel the cucumbers, cut down the centre and deseed with a little spoon. Slice. Melt the butter in a saucepan, add the cucumber, cook gently for 10 minutes. Stir in the flour until well mixed then gradually add the heated chicken stock, stirring constantly. Pour the milk through a strainer into the soup, discarding the onions. Simmer for 10 minutes, season, cool, liquidise in the blender. When cold stir in the cream, chill. Serve with chopped mint leaves.

Now here's a soup especially for you who have your own vegetable gardens where everything comes up in vast quantities at the same time, the lovely little peas at the pop and the lettuces imitating the Tower of Babel ever upwards.

———— *Pea and lettuce soup* ————

2 lbs of shelled young peas
2 hearts of cabbage lettuce
a good bunch of spring onions
4 oz butter

2 pints of water
$\frac{1}{2}$ pint thick cream
salt and sugar

Clean and slice the spring onions. Tear the lettuce into thin strips. Melt the butter in your soup saucepan, put in the spring onions, the shelled peas and the lettuce; sprinkle with two teaspoons of salt and two of sugar. Mix well, cover and cook gently for 15 minutes. Pour in the water, bring to the boil then simmer until the peas are quite tender. Cool, liquidise, add the cream, check the seasoning and chill. Serve with some chopped mint and maybe a scattering of very finely chopped ham. This is an exquisite soup; you can use frozen petits pois, but it ain't the same.

The other thing Clare wanted was a receipt for meringues, simple and safe. Here goes. For each egg white you need 2 oz of caster sugar. Whip egg whites stiffly until you can hold the bowl over your head upside-down without disaster. Whip in half the sugar then fold in the rest. Set the oven at the lowest temperature, like gas $\frac{1}{4}$. Line baking trays with that magic non-stick baking paper. With two teaspoons plop the mixtures in rows of four or five. Bake for an hour and a half. If there is more than one tray change the positions in the oven half way through.

9 May 1987

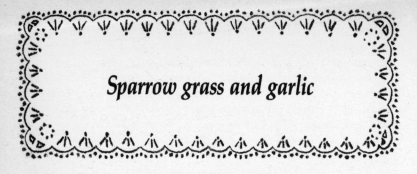

Sparrow grass and garlic

There seems to be an enormous amount of asparagus in the markets this year, of every size and very reasonably priced for once. I particularly like the thin little ones called sprue, they have a delicious flavour and seem to be the cheapest. Whatever size you choose to buy I think the best way of cooking them is to steam them, unless you have one of those grand asparagus kettles which cook them upright. I have a large Aga steamer which is admirable for the job, but a colander over a well-fitting saucepan should do as well. Make sure the stalks are grit-free under a running tap, but don't soak. Nothing is better than just eating asparagus in your fingers, having dipped them into whichever sauce you prefer; in Rome I have had them served with lightly fried eggs sprinkled with parmesan, you dip into the yolks leaving a disgusting debris of the whites. However if you have a surfeit of asparagus (happy thought) you could make:

——— Asparagus mousse ———

1 bunch of asparagus
½ pint of made-up aspic
4 hard-boiled eggs

¼ pint of thick cream
salt and pepper

Clean the asparagus, cut off the coarse part of the stalk and steam until tender. Drain off any excess water, then mash or liquidise them. Chop the boiled eggs fairly finely, whip the cream thick enough to leave a trail. Combine all the ingredients folding the cream in last, season with ground salt and pepper and pour into a suitable mould. Chill until set. Turn out and serve with more asparagus surrounding it, and maybe a light mayonnaise to dip into.

If you prefer something hot you could indulge in:

Asparagus soufflé

1 bunch of asparagus
3 oz butter
3 dessertspoons of plain flour
8 fluid oz milk
4 spring onions

1 clove, 1 bay leaf
3 large eggs
3 dessertspoons freshly grated
    parmesan cheese
salt, pepper, paprika and nutmeg

Chop the spring onions and place in a small saucepan with the milk, the clove and the bay leaf. Bring to the boil, take off the heat, leave to steep. Wash and trim the asparagus, leaving about five inches of the tender tips, steam until just tender, drain well and place in the bottom of a well-buttered soufflé dish. Melt the butter in a saucepan, add the flour, stirring until quite smooth but not browning. Add the strained milk little by little, stirring the while until all is amalgamated and at the boil. Remove from the heat to cool somewhat. Separate the eggs. Beat the yolks with a little salt and fresh-ground pepper, a pinch of paprika, a scrape of nutmeg and the parmesan cheese. Mix into the milk sauce. Beat the egg whites stiffly then fold them into the mixture with loving care. Pour over the asparagus. Place the dish in the middle of a pre-heated oven at Gas 7, 425° F, 218° C for 30 to 35 minutes.

The other great treat that has just appeared in the market is the succulent fresh garlic with its great cloves bursting from tender green and purple surrounds. I am totally addicted to it. Colin Spencer who also worships at the shrine of the 'sacred herb' has a stunning recipe for roasted garlic. Peel the cloves (he goes up to 200 for a family affair – wow!), toss in olive oil, season with salt and pepper, place in a covered earthenware dish in a preheated oven at medium heat for half an hour. Serve sprinkled with parsley. These, eaten with a simple bit of steak, lamb or chicken are stupendous and not at all strong.

Finally a dish of extreme simplicity:

Spaghetti with oil and garlic

1½ lbs of spaghetti (enough for six)
6 whole cloves of garlic
6 tablespoons of the best olive oil

black pepper
2 tablespoons of chopped parsley

Peel the cloves of garlic and fry them gently in the olive oil until golden yellow. Take the cloves out of the pan and throw them away. (This is the correct thing to do but I often leave them to eat.) Keep the oil boiling and pour sizzling over the prepared spaghetti. This sauce should be prepared at the last moment when the pasta is nearly ready.

As soon as the spaghetti are cooked, drain them not too dry and grind lots of black pepper over them then add the boiling oil and sprinkle with the parsley. Eat at once without cheese.

6 June 1987

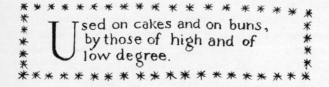

It's the flavour that counts

It's the colour that attracts

U sed on cakes and on buns, by those of high and of low degree.

Easy accessibility of all movable parts

Goodbye Gimson

We lost our dear Andrew Gimson last week, he of the cherubic face and maniacal laughter. He has gone off to Ireland and then to join the *Independent* and the other ex-*Spectator* figures; I think his wild trip to Majorca with the 18-30 Club has a lot to answer for. Before he left he had a farewell lunch with his own choice of guests and as it was suitably summery I shall use it for this piece.

First they had a good strong pâté based on one of Madam David's, no bacon, no pork, very simple, very good, quick and easy.

——— Chicken liver pâté ———

1 lb of chicken livers	thyme and garlic
4 oz of unsalted butter	salt and pepper
3 tablespoons of brandy (or whisky)	4 oz of butter for sealing
3 tablespoons of port (or cream sherry)	

It is nigh impossible to get fresh chicken livers in abundance but the frozen ones do very well for this. Melt them slowly and then drain them in a sieve. Remove any sinews and make sure that no little green bile sacs have been left behind. Melt half the unsalted butter in a frying pan, put in the chicken livers and cook gently for about five minutes, turning them over and over to cook evenly but leaving them pink within. Scoop them out with a perforated spoon and place in a mixer or processor. (Failing these you must just use a pestle and mortar and strength.) Return the pan and its juices to the heat, pour in the brandy, bring to the bubble, then add the port. Simmer for a minute or two. Season the livers with a little salt and quite a lot of freshly ground black pepper, add a peeled clove of garlic, a good-sized one, and a fair pinch of thyme. Blend into a paste. Pour in the juices from the pan and add the remaining 2 oz of unsalted butter. Blend again until smooth and well mixed. Place this mixture in a suitable terrine or soufflé dish, leaving enough room to seal with butter. Chill the pâté for a bit until set. Melt about 4 oz of butter in a pan, then pour it through a sieve over the pâté to seal it. Keep in the refrigerator for three days before eating. Serve well chilled with hot toast. Plenty for eight people.

The next course was a fine sea trout. These creatures are plentiful and excellent at the moment. Mine was a six-pounder, which I cooked in a fish kettle, but the smaller ones from two to four pounds are more suitable for the average table. Simply oil a large sheet of foil, place the fish in the middle, season liberally with salt and pepper. Twist the foil together to make a loose parcel, place it on a baking tray and cook in a preheated oven at Gas 4, 335° F, 179° C for 40 minutes, take out and leave to cool in the foil. If you want it hot put a small glass of dry vermouth over the fish before parcelling and add another 5 minutes to the cooking time. Serve with new potatoes and a good home-made mayonnaise to which you have added a plentiful chopping of chives, parsley and tarragon. A plain cucumber salad is the usual accompaniment but I have just made a turnip and cucumber salad at home which was a bit different and to my mind delicious with the rich trout.

———— *Turnip and cucumber salad* ————

a cucumber
6–8 small French turnips
1 fat clove of fresh garlic
olive oil

lemon juice
dill
salt and pepper

Peel the cucumber in stripes, leaving some of the green skin. Slice, salt and put between two plates with a weight on top to drain for an hour. The turnips are those ravishing little white and purple creatures which are about at the moment; they have a lovely peppery flavour. Peel them and boil whole in salted water until just tender but not soft, from 10 to 15 minutes. Drain well, place in a bowl and immediately coat with olive oil, season with salt and ground pepper and some lemon juice; mix in the garlic, finely chopped. Leave to cool, then slice to match the cucumber. Squeeze the remaining moisture from the cucumber, mix with the turnips and sprinkle with a lot of chopped dill. Check the seasoning, adding more olive oil and lemon juice. If you were eating this salad with less rich fare you could smother it with sour cream which is a lovely combination.

So farewell, Gimson, we shall love you and miss you.

4 July 1987

Cold comfort

I am writing from Cumberland, where the sauce does not come from, just outside Cockermouth, gazing across billiard-green lawns and parkland tastefully dotted with cows. It is pouring with rain of course, but very lush. I vainly hope for sun, to go swimming in the glorious lakes, but it has evaded me for the last few years. I am on an annual visit for the broad bean season; quite one of the best vegetables in the world, taken straight from the garden into the pot. My beloved host, Patricius Senhouse, picks everything very young, so the deliciousness of the beans cannot be overstated; they are a dream. This is a dish he uses as a first course and very excellent it is.

Broad beans Fitz

1½ lbs shelled young broad beans
6 rashers of streaky bacon –
    unsmoked
4 hard-boiled eggs

a tin-and-a-half of anchovies
chives and parsley
olive oil, lemon juice, salt and pepper

Make a dressing with about 5 oz of the best olive oil, lemon juice, salt and fresh-ground black pepper to suit your own taste, but keep it slightly tart. Cut the bacon into smallish bits and put under the grill until quite crisp (or fry). Leave to drain on some paper towelling. Put the beans into boiling salted water until just tender, drain in a colander, rushing cold water over them for a moment or two to 'refresh'. The hard-boiled eggs should have been peeled and left in cold water until you need them, this stops them getting that horrendous green outline round the yolks. Pat them dry and chop roughly; mix with a good amount of the parsley and chives chopped fairly finely. Lay the beans in some pretty china dish and sprinkle with the bacon pieces, pile the eggs and herbs on top and lattice the whole with the anchovy fillets. Chill slightly. Just before serving, pour the dressing all over the beans and bring to table with some good crusty bread or toast.

I have discovered that if you are going to have roast beef or lamb for some meal there is no need to do it just in time. I do it the night before, thus obviating all that last-minute sweating over the oven and leaving nasty greasy oven pans in the sink when you need them most. It doesn't matter whether you are serving the meat as a hot repast or a cold one, the meat will taste much better, having saved all its juices within rather than pouring them out on the carving board. It will be easier to carve and the leftovers will be as good as the original. There is nothing more depressing than the sight of an old joint that has been carved when hot then left to grow sad and grey in the larder. If you are intending to serve it cold, well and good. If hot just pretend that it is. Served on hot plates with the accompanying hot vegetables and gravy made from the deglazing of the oven pan (also done the night before and kept up your sleeve) no one will notice. When you consider that a hot joint should have 'rested' 20 minutes before serving and then all the time taken in carving and serving, the actual meat is never all that hot anyway.

The best way to roast is to have a grid in the pan allowing the heat to flow evenly around the joint, which should really not be less than 4 lbs in weight for satisfactory cooking. Place the meat on the grid having smeared it with oil and put in a preheated oven at Gas 9, 475° F, 250° C, for quarter of an hour then turn down to Gas 4, 360° F, 185° C, for the rest of the time. Do beef for $\frac{1}{4}$-hour a pound and for lamb add an extra $\frac{1}{4}$-hour. Half way through, salt and flavour the joint with herbs, garlic, Worcester sauce or what you will. Leave to cool on the grid. This will produce nicely red beef and rosy pink lamb.

Another treat we are having at the moment is masses of raspberries from the garden, great big beautiful creatures. Here is an outrageously simple thing to do with them. Make a batch of meringues. Half fill a pudding bowl with whipped cream, stir in as many raspberries as you see fit, crush some of the meringues and mix them in, then cover the top with some whole ones. Heavenly bunch of textures, crunchy and sloppy.

8 August 1987

Cocktail capers

I am so cold at this moment of writing I yearn for hot comforting winter dishes which I shall indulge in below.

The dry martini cocktail, though very delicious, is a pernicious lethal drink but the ingredients of gin and dry vermouth produce an excellent flavour in stews, casseroles and the like. I know gin is not used in Provence but it is more usual in the average British household and does very well.

Daube de boeuf à la Provençale

3 lbs of good stewing steak
8 thick slices of streaky fresh pork
14 oz of chopped tomatoes (fresh or tinned)
$\frac{1}{2}$ lb sliced mushrooms
beef stock
olive oil

12 oz dry vermouth, 3 oz gin
thyme, bay leaf, 4 fat cloves of garlic
1 lb thinly sliced carrots
1 lb thinly sliced onions
salt, pepper, plain flour
Dijon mustard
capers, parsley

Cut the meat into $2\frac{1}{2}$ inch squares, one inch thick. Place in a roomy bowl. Add two tablespoons of olive oil, the gin and vermouth, two crushed cloves of garlic, the bay leaf and thyme, the sliced carrots and onions, two teaspoons of Malden salt and a goodly grinding of black pepper. Mix this marinade with the meat for six hours or overnight, turning and basting at intervals. Put about 3 oz of flour into a plastic bag, season with salt and pepper, remove beef from the marinade and toss in the flour, about five pieces at a time, lay them on some grease-proof paper. Put the mushrooms and drained tomatoes into the marinade. Lay half the pork slices on the bottom of a suitably sized casserole, cover with a third of the vegetable mixture then alternate with layers of meat and vegetables. Place the remaining pork slices on top and any marinade that is left. Heat on top of the stove to simmering point, cook for 20 minutes covered. Have a look to see if the meat is now just covered by liquid, if not top up with beef stock. Pre-heat the oven to Gas 2, 325° F, 163° C; put the casserole in the lower part and simmer slowly for three to four hours until the meat is tender when pierced. Bring to the top of the stove and taste for seasoning. If you want to thicken the liquid, scoop about half a pint out and mix with a dessert spoon of cornflour into a smooth consistency, boil for two minutes then stir back into the daube: but it shouldn't be necessary. While the meat has been cooking crush the remaining two cloves of garlic into a mortar with three tablespoons of drained capers, pound into a paste then beat in three tablespoons of strong Dijon mustard and gradually three tablespoons of olive oil as you would for mayonnaise. Mix in a good handful of chopped parsley. Stir into the finished daube just before serving.

Another use for the martini mixture is with pork chops. Gin is always good with pork on account of the juniper flavouring.

———— Gin and French pork chops ————

4 pork chops
2 oz of gin
2 oz of dry vermouth
lemon juice
olive oil

10 cloves of garlic, thyme, bay leaf
2 oz butter
salt and pepper
capers

Get good thick chops with some fat and rind on them. Place in shallow dish. Cut one of the cloves of garlic into tiny slithers and press into the chops near the bone. Sprinkle with lemon juice, gin and vermouth; crumble the bay leaf and some thyme over them, season with ground salt and pepper, libate with about two tablespoons of olive oil. Leave to marinate for at least two hours tossing and turning at will. Throw the rest of the garlic into boiling water for two minutes, drain, cool, peel and chop roughly. Melt the butter in a thick heavy frying pan. Scrape the marinade off the chops (reserving every drop) pat them dryish and brown quickly on each side to seal them. Lower the heat, add the chopped garlic, cover the pan and cook very gently for half an hour turning over at half time or you could put them into a moderate oven if it suited you. When tender transfer to a warm dish. Pour the marinade into the juices of the pan, let them bubble, taste for seasoning, add two tablespoons of capers, pour over the chops. Serve with mashed potatoes and endive salad.

In answer to doubting Jill Simmons (Letters, 22 August) of course I wouldn't serve coley as salmon, they are different colours, although I have had folk think my egg mousse flavoured with paprika was salmon mousse so who knows? However, many thanks for the interest.

5 September 1987

Simply Ladenis

A little helpful hint to start with. I have noticed in friends' houses where the ice is made in the freezer part of the refrigerator that due to spillage or leaky ice trays the freezing base gets to resemble the icy wastes of the North Pole, all jagged ice rocks and lumps which make for more frozen spillage each time you put the trays back. Next time you defreeze find a suitably sized plastic tray to hold the ice trays, then when it gets iced up you simply take it out, rinse off and return, instead of the dreary de-freezing process.

I have been reading the wonderful *My Gastronomy* by the splendid Nico Ladenis and thought to pick out some of his more simple receipts for you. Digby Anderson will give it a proper review, I believe, but here are a few foretastes. As Ladenis is a restaurateur most of the dishes are for two, so you must just multiply at will.

———— *Escalopes of fresh salmon in chive sauce* ————

8 oz fresh salmon
1 tablespoon fruity olive oil
salt and cayenne pepper

$6\frac{1}{2}$ tablespoons of the chive sauce per helping
1 tablespoon of chopped chives

Slice the salmon very thinly using the same technique as for smoked salmon. Put the slices in the middle of a heat-proof gratin dish (Ladenis says two good porcelain plates but this frightens me). Brush the slices with the oil and arrange untidily overlapping each other. They look rather tidy in the yummy illustration but there you are. Dust very

99

lightly with the salt and cayenne pepper. Surround with the chive sauce and sprinkle with the chopped chives and place in a very hot pre-heated oven Gas 9, 475° F, 240° C for three to five minutes. Do not allow the salmon to be overcooked and dry. Serve with a good dry white burgundy.

Now for the sauce. This makes 1–1½ pints.

—————— *Sauce crème de ciboulette* ———–—

7 fluid oz white fish stock
3 fluid oz Noilly Prat vermouth
2 fluid oz good white burgundy
4 oz finely chopped shallots
4 oz finely chopped leeks (the white part)

17 fluid oz double cream
2 fluid oz sauternes
2 tablespoons of chopped chives
2 oz sliced butter
salt and pepper

Put the fish stock, vermouth, white burgundy and shallots in a stainless steel pan and reduce over a moderate heat to four tablespoons. Place the chopped leeks and ¼ pint of water in another pan and reduce to two tablespoons. Pass this through a fine sieve into the first pan. Add the cream, the sauternes and 1½ tablespoons of chopped chives, bring to the boil then whisk in the sliced butter until it melts entirely. Season and strain carefully. Scatter the remaining chives just before serving.

Here is a way to make those rather tasteless little poussins really delicious.

————— *[Poussins with muscatel grape brandy]* —————
(l'Eau de Vie de Frontignan)

2 corn-fed poussins
2 oz butter
6 rashers of bacon
pepper and salt

¼ pint rich port
2 teaspoons tomato purée
2 teaspoons finely chopped tarragon
2–4 tablespoons muscatel brandy

Smear the birds all over with butter and sprinkle with fresh-ground pepper. Wrap three rashers of bacon round each creature. Roast in a heavy cast-iron pan in a pre-heated oven Gas 8, 450° F, 230° C for 20 minutes. Turn the oven down to Gas 5, 375° F, 190° C. Push the bacon off the birds into the bottom of the pan, baste and cook the birds for another ten minutes. Remove the birds and keep warm.

Discard the bacon and pour off the fat. Add the port to the pan, bring to the boil and stir in the tomato purée, simmer until the sauce becomes syrupy, season with salt and pepper, mix in the tarragon; bring back to the boil then add the brandy, stir quickly then pour over the poussins which you could have dismembered or split in two according to your tastes. Garnish with some fine muscatel grapes. Serve with a fruity, medium-dry white wine or a slightly chilled young fruity red.

Two medium carrots sliced finely on a mandoline cooked in a tablespoon of reduced chicken stock, 2 oz of butter and 1 teaspoon of honey for seven minutes then seasoned with salt and pepper would be excellent with these birds.

3 October 1987

Bones of content

I seem to have been doing the rounds of raw or smoked salmon viewing this past month. The Scottish Salmon Board was giving lessons on how to carve smoked salmon, and there was a wonderful display of Japanese knife dexterity with raw salmon at David Queensberry's studios, a riveting performance of expertise, a joy to watch, apart from being quite delicious to eat, dunked into a mixture of Japanese soy sauce and their incredibly hot green horse-radish.

Then yesterday, Sunday lunch at the ubiquitous Anthony Blond's, where they had gathered most of the great chefs of London. Jonathan Meades from the *Times* produced raw slices of salmon anointed with hazelnut oil, sprinkled with some very exotic pepper and topped with frizzled particles of the salmon skin – wonderful.

However, today as I write is the feast of All Souls, so I thought an Italian confection called Dead Men's Bones would be appropriate. They are always made in the shape of a shin-bone.

——— *Osse dei morti* ———

2 egg whites
2½ oz icing sugar
3 oz good plain chocolate
1 oz semolina
4 oz blanched almonds

For the icing:
3 oz of plain chocolate
¾ oz unsalted butter

Line a couple of baking trays with rice paper and pre-heat the oven to Gas 2, 300° F, 154° C. Grate the first lot of chocolate finely and cut the almonds into strips. Whisk the egg whites until stiff, add half the sugar, continue whisking until shiny. Fold in the rest of the sugar, the grated chocolate, the semolina and the almonds all with a light touch. Spoon the mixture in long bone-like shapes onto the rice-papered trays, fairly well apart. Flatten slightly with a wet knife, then bake in the middle of the oven for 25 minutes until light brown and dry. Leave to cool for about ten minutes, then transfer to a wire rack.

Make the icing by melting the broken-up remaining chocolate in a little basin over simmering water; stir in the butter, mixing well. When the 'bones' are quite cold spread the rice-paper side of each with the icing and make wavy lines down them with the prongs of a fork. Leave to set. These are very good munched with a creamy pudding and wine.

Now to other bones. My uncle has been pilgrimaging in Jerusalem, so I have been cooking the things I love and he hates, boiled gelatinous things like oxtail and pigs' trotters. I get four handsome trotters for 50 pence; they must be the cheapest meat on the market. My favourite method is the breadcrumbed one giving the lovely crisp outside to crunch through before hitting the gelatinous centre.

Pieds de porc panés

4 pigs' trotters
1 large onion
3 carrots
2 leeks
2 sticks of celery

big bunch of parsley and a bay leaf
a good strip of lemon peel
a few cloves
homemade toasted breadcrumbs
melted butter

Sprinkle the trotters with salt a few hours or the night before cooking, then rinse off. Put them in a large saucepan with all the vegetables roughly sliced, the herbs and a little salt. Cover with cold water, bring to the boil, cover and simmer very gently for six hours (ideal if you are an Aga owner). Take the trotters from the pan carefully with a perforated implement. Leave to cool, removing any bones that seem to be falling out. Place between two boards with a weight on top until quite cold. Brush them all over with melted butter, then roll in fine toasted breadcrumbs. They are now ready to be grilled at will to heat them through and give them a crunchy coating. Alternatively, you can warm them up in the oven, then finish off under a fiercer grill. They should be piping hot. Serve with a sauce tartare, ravigote or remoulade. I prefer the remoulade. Pound two hard egg yolks with a touch of white wine vinegar, add a raw yolk, a teaspoon of strong Dijon mustard, salt and pepper, then beat in about a quarter pint of excellent olive oil as for mayonnaise. Stir in a teaspoon each of chopped tarragon, chives, capers and parsley.

The liquid from the trotters boiled up again with some shin of beef will produce a splendid jellied stock.

7 November 1987

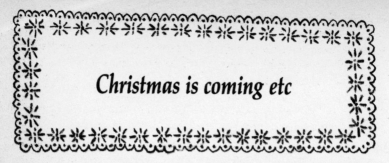

Christmas is coming etc

Advent already and all those terrible teddy bears lighting up Regent Street; whoever heard of the Teddy Bears' Christmas? Prince Edward outdid himself screaming, 'Let there be light,' as he switched the little horrors on. That was not what the Deity meant at all, I wonder if His Royal Highness realised that. He said it was a well-known phrase or words to that effect. Away dull gloom, let joy be abounding as well as food and drink and all the best to Madam Currie.

I love scallops as well as any shellfish; the following receipt would be an appropriate and appetising dish for Christmas Eve.

—— Scallops with leeks ——

12 scallops on their shells
8 young leeks, about a lb
2 shallots
$\frac{1}{4}$ pint thick cream
2 oz of butter

a bunch of parsley (flat-leafed if possible)
4 tablespoons of dry vermouth
$\frac{1}{4}$ pint of dry white wine
pepper and salt

Get the fishmonger to detach the little creatures from their shells. Separate the white flesh from the corals. Remove the hard surround of the white and the tiny black sac from the coral. Wash clean under a running tap. Cut the whites in two horizontally. Leave to drain and dry a bit. Wash the leeks, cut off the green parts (use them for soup or stocks). Slice the white stems in half, then into narrow strips about two inches long, and place in a saucepan with one ounce of the butter, a pinch of salt and eight tablespoons of water. Cover and simmer for 20 minutes. Keep hot. Melt the remaining butter in another saucepan, chop the shallots fine, cook gently until soft. Add the scallops and their corals, the wine and the vermouth. Bring to the boil, turn the heat low, simmer for just two minutes. With a slotted instrument remove the leeks from their liquid, place in a heated dish then place the scallops and corals on top, also using the slotted spoon for them. Add the leek juice to the scallop juice, bring to the boil and cook briskly until the liquid is reduced to eight tablespoons. Pour in the cream, bring back to the boil, let it bubble a moment or two, adjust the seasoning with salt and several grinds of the peppermill, and pour the lot over the scallops and leeks. This is really delicious and would be enough for four to six people, depending on the size of the fish and the appetites of the folk.

If you decide to have a goose for Christmas this stuffing of prunes is very delectable, more adventurous than the apple ones.

Prune and foie gras stuffing

50 prunes; tea
$\frac{1}{4}$ pint of dry vermouth
$\frac{3}{4}$ pint of goose stock (made from the neck and giblets)
the goose's liver finely chopped
4 shallots finely chopped

1 oz butter
$\frac{1}{4}$ pint of port
4 oz of good liver pâté
pinch of allspice and thyme
3 tablespoons of fresh breadcrumbs
salt and pepper

Soak the prunes in hot tea, leave until soft. Stone them. Place in a saucepan with the vermouth and stock, bring to the boil and simmer for ten minutes until tender. Strain them but keep the liquid. Fry the goose's liver and the shallots with the butter in a little frying-pan for two minutes, turn into a mixing bowl which will hold all the ingredients. Boil the port in the same pan until reduced to two tablespoons, scrape and add to the liver mixture. Beat the liver pâté, breadcrumbs, allspice, and thyme together, add to the rest, mixing thoroughly. Season with salt and pepper, then stir in the prunes. Salt the cavity of the goose, fill loosely with the stuffing and sew up the vent. For a 9 lb, oven-ready goose, preheat the oven to Gas 7, 425° F, 218° C. Prick the skin all over and see that it is dry. Roast breast side up for 15 minutes, lower heat to Gas 4, 350° F, 177° C, turn the goose onto its side. Baste every 20 minutes with three tablespoons of boiling water and remove excess fat from the pan into a bowl. The easiest way for both these operations is to use a bulb baster (the thing that looks like a sinister douching instrument). Halfway through the cooking, turn the goose onto its other side and finally on to its back for the last 15 minutes. The whole thing should be ready in $2\frac{1}{2}$ hours. Test by piercing the thigh; the juice should be pale yellow. Use the prune liquid to make the gravy, adding it to the pan roasting juices, having removed the fat. Treasure the goose fat for subsequent use.

5 December 1987

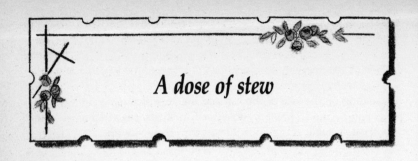

A dose of stew

'How weary, stale, flat and unprofitable seem to me all the uses of this world,' or in other words I am completely struck down with flu for the first time in 20 years, feel ghastly and can't get it together too well so please bear with me. The idea of food simply does not figure, all I seem to want is gallons of water (very unlike me) and some fruit pastilles left over from *Little Dorrit* which have been a great comfort to me. Bovril is a comfort but nothing else. I have a friend going on 60 who at the first sign that all is not well with the body goes straight to bed with toast and honey and all the Beatrix Potter books. That's his comfort, perhaps we all have our own.

As I am not up to anything inventive I shall give you a couple of good wintry receipts that were contained in a dear little book advertising Le Creuset ware years ago given by Madam David.

Shin of beef stewed in red wine

2½ lbs shin of beef (fat and skin removed)
4 oz fat salt pork or bacon (in one piece)
olive oil
1 large onion
2 cloves of garlic
thyme and bayleaf
2 tablespoons of plain flour
½ pint of red wine
½ pint of meat stock
salt and pepper

I love shin of beef for stews, it is after all osso bucco grown up and produces that lovely sticky, slightly gelatinous texture and has a splendid flavour (real beef tea for instance). Cut the salt pork into cubes leaving the rind on. If using bacon remove rind. Put the cubes and two tablespoons of olive oil into a casserole that will hold all the ingredients, heat gently until the fat starts oozing then add the sliced onion letting it slowly take colour. Cut the meat in good size strips, season with salt and fresh ground pepper and sprinkle with the flour. Put the meat into the casserole mixing well with the onion and pork. Heat the wine in a saucepan then pour it bubbling over the meat. Boil fiercely for a moment. Add the meat stock. Place the bayleaf, sprigs of thyme and crushed garlic cloves in the middle of the meat, cover the pot and place in a preheated low oven Gas 1, 290° F, 143° C for about three hours or you can cook it for half the time one day and finish it off the next if more convenient. Just before serving taste for seasoning and leave to bubble on top of the stove to reduce the sauce a little. Serve with potato purée. An alternative method for the stew is to use instead of the wine and stock, a couple of tablespoons each of port and mushroom ketchup and half a pint of stout, also the addition of half a pound of chopped-up ox kidney with the meat. Otherwise make a:

———— Casserole of kidney and mushrooms ————

1 lb of ox kidney
2 tablespoons of plain flour
3 oz of butter
8 fluid oz of port or red wine (or mixed)

$\frac{1}{2}$ lb of mushrooms
mustard, salt and pepper

Put the kidney to soak in a bowl of warm, slightly salted water for at least 30 minutes or over night or day if so it suits you. Drain the kidney, pat dry with some kitchen towel then cut into slices a quarter of an inch thick. Sprinkle with salt, freshly ground pepper and the flour. Melt the butter in a suitably sized casserole, put in the kidneys. Cook very gently for five minutes stirring them round the pan. Little by little add the port or wine, let it come to simmering point then let it bubble for a minute. Cover and place in a pre-heated low oven Gas 1, 290° F, 143° C for an hour. At this stage add the mushrooms, wiped clean but left whole. Return to the oven for a further half-hour.

Just before serving, make some strong English mustard and stir a dessert spoonful into the kidney dish. Serve with good mashed potatoes flavoured with a scrap of lemon peel or with plain boiled rice.

Both these dishes can be started the day before but don't buy or use the mushrooms until the last moment necessary.

I trust none of you will get this wretched flu but if you do I have discovered a new pastille which seems very efficacious for a honking cough, especially if kept stuck to the top palate over night. They are called Hill's Bronchial Balsam Pastilles and rejoice in the legend 'PLEASANT – BUT REALLY POTENT'. I'm hooked.

23 January 1988

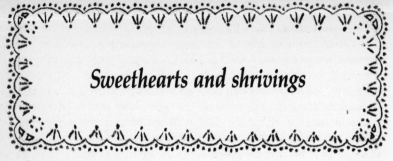

Sweethearts and shrivings

A week full of incident awaits us. Sunday will be dear old and banished Valentine's day, and Tuesday is 'Shrove' pancake day when a lot of curious races and traditional rites take place. Even Westminster School gets into some messy fight over the delicacy. Cooks used to keep their first six pancakes as an offering: 'One for Peter, two for Paul and three for Him who made us all.' Isn't that quaint? The next day will be Ash Wednesday, the first day of Lent and time for the big Fatso Fast. I thought you might celebrate St Valentine's with artichoke hearts, making a beautiful dish for your beloved.

Using one large artichoke per beloved, cook in boiling water with the addition of two tablespoons of white wine vinegar or lemon juice for about 40 minutes. They are cooked when the outer leaves pull off easily. Drain thoroughly upside-down until cool enough to handle. Discard any nasty little leaves. Pluck off the good leaves and arrange neatly around personal plates or on a huge platter, depending on the amount of people. Remove the hairy choke carefully with a teaspoon, rub each heart with lemon juice and place in the centre of the leaves so that they rather resemble a green sunflower. Fill the hearts with hollandaise sauce or good homemade mayonnaise, place two or three hard-boiled quail's eggs on these little nests, sprinkle with paprika and serve with more sauce on the side for dipping. An obvious labour of love and stunning to behold. For Shrove Tuesday, go grand and old-fashioned and make the Queen of the Pancakes:

——— Crêpes Suzette ———

For the crêpes:
¼ lb of plain flour
large pinch of salt
½ pint of milk and water
2 eggs
2 oz unsalted butter

For the sauce:
2 oz cube sugar
2 large oranges
2 oz unsalted butter
1 tbsp of Cointreau or Grand Marnier
2 tablespoons brandy

Mix the flour and salt in a large bowl, make a well in the centre. Beat in the eggs and half the milk and water with a wooden spoon until quite smooth; add the rest of the liquid. The mixture should be the thickness of cream. Leave to rest for 30 minutes if possible. Using a six-inch frying pan with a heavy bottom, make 12 small pancakes, using the butter for frying, a tiny amount each time. Pour the batter in with a gravy ladle, just enough to cover the base of the pan, fry gently on both sides (toss if you dare) until golden brown. Keep warm on a covered plate over a saucepan of simmering water as you proceed. Rub the sugar cubes over the oranges until they are bright yellow from the zest. Crush and put into a big frying pan with a tablespoon of water, dissolve gently then simmer/boil until golden brown. Add the juice from the oranges until all is melted together, then gradually the butter and the liqueur. Reheat the pancakes separately in the sauce. Once in, fold each one in four and push to the side. When they are all in the pan pour the brandy (heated) over them, set ablaze and serve immediately.

Finally, for Ash Wednesday and onward:

——— *Lenten leek tart* ———

An eight-inch flan ring, ready with a
    short or quiche pastry case blind
    baked
3 lbs leeks
1 large clove of garlic
3 egg yolks

$\frac{1}{4}$ pint thick cream
2 oz freshly grated parmesan cheese
salt, pepper, nutmeg
2 oz butter

Clean and slice the white part of the leeks and the garlic, let them melt gently in a pan with the butter. Spread the mixture into the pastry flan. Beat the egg yolks and cream, add the parmesan and season with freshly ground pepper, salt and grated nutmeg. Pour over the leeks and dot with pieces of butter. Bake in a preheated oven at Gas 4, 350° F, 180° C for 30 to 40 minutes until firm and golden — serve after ten minutes' rest.

13 February 1988

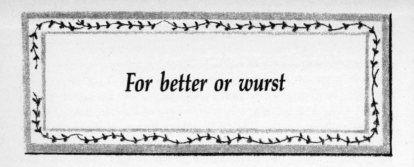

For better or wurst

I am not really into Hun food. I don't think they really have a cuisine, what they have is a lot of good produce and 1,500 types of sausage which they eat for breakfast, lunch and dinner in one way or another. Great platters of mixed sliced sausage and cheese for breakfast; lunch tends to be their main meal with enormous casseroles incorporating more sausage and knuckles of pork or veal: then in the evening more cold cuts with salads, soups, dumplings and potato dishes followed by some rich tart or pudding.

There are also quite a lot of smoked and cooked hams and cured loin of pork. The Westphalian ham is the German equivalent to Italian Parma ham and though very good in its way is soundly trumped for deliciousness by the Italian. The same goes for the salami family.

Enormous amounts of butter are produced every year, and it is apparently available throughout Britain, though I have never knowingly seen it. Perhaps it is disguised as Sainsbury's or Waitrose. Then there are a lot of rather soapy cheeses to be eaten with all those soured breads, as well as the fake camembert and brie which compare with our filthy Lymeswold.

I have been down to the German Food Centre, 44–46 Knightsbridge, London SW1, which is bursting with all this produce as well as masses of cakes and chocolates. There are wonderful things for Easter if you are in search of eggs, bunnies or chickens in sweet form.

Cabbage is another great favourite whether it be 'sauer' or 'fresh'. Here is a receipt for:

——— Stuffed cabbage leaves ———

8 large cabbage leaves
3 oz long grain rice
2 onions, finely chopped
1 tablespoon cooking oil

7 oz German *Quark* (cream cheese)
$\frac{1}{2}$ teaspoon mixed herbs
a good pinch of caraway seeds
salt and pepper

5 oz German liver sausage	For the sauce:
1 oz raisins	$\frac{3}{4}$ pint tomato juice
1 oz almonds, chopped	3 tablespoons sour cream

Blanch the cabbage leaves by plunging them into boiling salted water for five minutes, then drain them. Cook the rice in six fluid oz of boiling salted water for 12 minutes until tender, drain. Fry the onions in the oil until lightly browned, mix into the rice and stir in the chopped liver sausage, *Quark*, raisins and almonds. Add sufficient tomato juice to give a thick but soft consistency. Season with the herbs, caraway seeds, salt and freshly ground pepper. Divide the mixture into eight portions, place each portion on a cabbage leaf and make them into little parcels. You may need the help of a cocktail stick. Put the parcels into a shallow ovenproof dish, pour over the rest of the tomato juice and the sour cream. Cover and bake in a preheated oven at Gas 4, 150° F, 180° C, for 45 to 50 minutes.

I obtained the following receipt from Hilda Podiebrad, an old friend who came over from Berlin after the war. It is an assembly cake, no cooking, and she has made it for years as a treat for children or even on a mammoth scale for wedding cakes when the children had grown up. The essential ingredient is the coconut butter.

——— *Kalte Torte or Cold dog* ———

2 medium eggs	$\frac{1}{2}$ lb of coconut butter (Palmin or
10 tablespoons caster sugar	Cofetta)
2 tablespoons icing sugar	$\frac{1}{2}$ lb packet of petit beurre biscuits
6 tablespoons real cocoa powder	

Line a loaf tin $9\frac{1}{4}'' \times 5\frac{1}{4}'' \times 2\frac{3}{4}''$ (approx) with greaseproof paper. Beat the eggs until creamy, add both the sugars and the cocoa, mix well and smoothly, using a hand electric mixer if available. Melt the coconut butter in a small saucepan but do not allow to boil. Slowly add to the mixture, beating the while. You can add a few drops of rum, coffee or vanilla to taste. Pour a thin layer of this confection into the base of the loaf tin, then cover with a layer of the petit beurre biscuits; continue these layers, finishing with a chocolate one. Chill in the refrigerator until needed. Turn out and serve in thin slices. Very rich.

You can purchase the Cofetta at the German Food Centre, and they swear it is the same thing as Palmin, doing the same job, otherwise I dare say Selfridges stocks it as well for the German season.

19 March 1988

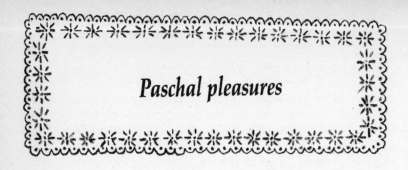

Paschal pleasures

I hope you all had a perfectly splendid Easter. We did very well in London, with blazing sunshine from Good Friday onwards, hot enough to sit in the garden for pre-prandial drinks on Easter Sunday, whetting our appetites for the Paschal Lamb which was delicious, cooked with many root vegetables by kind friends. Left-over lamb is not a very pretty sight but this receipt adapted from Madam David is not only good, and, as she says, 'one of the most comforting dishes in the world', but also very topical for the wonderful exhibition at the British Museum. Go to the treasures first then return home for:

—— Suliman's pilaff ——

1 lb (2 cupfuls) of long grain rice
4 cupfuls of light stock or water
good dripping or best olive oil
the left-over lamb
2 biggish onions
2 cloves of garlic

1 14 oz tin of chopped tomatoes
2 oz of raisins
2 oz of currants
a handful of pine nuts or roasted
   almonds

Put four tablespoons of dripping or oil into a good saucepan with a tight fitting lid, heat the fat, stir in the rice until thoroughly coated, pour in the heated stock or water salted to taste, bring to simmering point, cover and leave for 20 minutes on a low heat by which time it should be cooked having used up all the liquid. Meanwhile chop the lamb into small pieces, sauté the onions cut into rings in the oil or dripping until soft and just browning then mix in the rest of the ingredients, fry the lot until heated through, season strongly. Combine with the rice and serve piping hot with yoghurt or sour cream on the side. Don't worry about the exact quantities, just use what you have. That is the point.

I was reminded of a very rich crab dish that I haven't cooked for years, I can't imagine why, the memory slips I suppose. It is very good indeed.

—— Crab gratin ——

1 lb of mixed crab meat (frozen or fresh)
4 oz of unsalted butter
¾ pint of double cream

2 tablespoons of medium sherry
freshly grated parmesan cheese
1 onion
parsley, salt and pepper

Chop the onion quite finely, fry gently in the butter until soft. Using a largish frying pan, pour in the cream, simmer carefully until the quantity is reduced by half (the larger frying pan facilitates this operation), add the sherry, season with fresh ground pepper and a drop or so of tabasco if you like. Be careful with the salt, remembering the cheese to come. Put the crab meat (defrosted if frozen) into a nice fireproof gratin dish, smooth it down evenly and cover with the hot cream sauce; sprinkle with about two tablespoons of the parmesan cheese. Place in a hot preheated oven and brown quickly. Serve with hot brown toast.

Finally, I thought you might like a pudding, thus making a full meal. I love prunes, such a good flavour and not used often enough.

—— Prune mousse ——

½ lb good quality prunes
1 lemon
2 oz caster sugar
½ oz gelatine

3 tablespoons port, or sherry or the like
½ pint double cream
Earl Grey tea

Make a pot of tea and pour it over the prunes lying in some suitable receptacle. Leave to soak overnight. Put the prunes into a saucepan with a half pint of the liquid and the lemon rind very thinly pared and cut into strips. Simmer until plump and tender, about 20 minutes. Take off the heat, add sugar, stir until dissolved. Strain the prunes but keep their juice. Stone the fruit and blend into a purée, mix with the juice of the lemon. Reheat the prune juice to simmering point, add the gelatine, stir like mad until dissolved, but never let it boil. Add to the prunes mixing evenly, flavour with the port, leave to cool. Whip the cream until light and fluffy, fold into the prune mixture, transfer to a dainty dish and chill in the refrigerator until set and ready for use. Serve with some lovely little sweet biscuits or those tiny macaroons.

9 April 1988

May munchings

Another grey, gloomy May-day Bank Holiday has gone by; I wish they would stop it or move it to a more cheerful moment. However, on the joyous side I have found a wonderful use for malt vinegar at last. It removes those stains in the bath, sink or lavatories caused by years of dripping hard water. You simply soak an old flannel or rag in vinegar, slap it on the offending marks, leave overnight or day and, hey presto! they disappear. I thought you might like to have this gem of information.

I was rooting through an old cigar box this week and found a receipt from Bumble Dawson, now dead alas. She designed clothes for films and stage but was a terrific food lover and cook. I once found Dirk Bogarde sitting next to me at lunch in her flat. Fancy! This is a suitably springtime receipt I feel.

——— *Cold parmesan soufflé* ———

3 large eggs
3 oz freshly grated parmesan cheese
1 teaspoon of Dijon mustard

a good pinch of cayenne pepper
$\frac{1}{2}$ pint of double cream
salt

I beg of you to use fresh parmesan, the packeted stuff just won't do. Separate the egg yolks from the whites. Beat the yolks until creamy. Add the cheese, Dijon, cayenne and a little salt to make a smooth paste. Whip the cream until thick and fluffy but not too hard. Beat about three spoonfuls into the cheese paste to soften it then fold the rest of the cream in with a light touch. Whisk the egg whites into stiff peaks and fold into the mixture (so start the egg yolks and cheese in a big enough bowl to accept all these ingredients). Turn into a soufflé dish, place in the refrigerator and chill all day.

Another good springtime dish is for poussins. They don't have a lot of flavour, poor little things, but this method gingers them up a treat.

Poussins with orange

2 plump poussins
2 oz of butter
½ pint of chicken stock
1 dessert spoon of plain flour
the grated rind and juice of a medium
    orange

1 dessert spoon of Dijon mustard
1 tablespoon of double cream
salt and pepper

Melt an ounce of the butter in a casserole that will contain the birds snugly. Place the creatures within and coat all over with the butter. Pour a quarter pint of the stock over them, season with salt and fresh ground pepper, cover and cook in a pre-heated oven at Gas 4, 355° F, 179° C, for 20 to 30 minutes. Remove the birds to cool a little then split them in two and remove the backbone. Arrange skin side up in another suitable dish for grilling. Put the original casserole over a moderate heat, stir in the flour, blending until quite smooth, add the rest of the stock, cook for a few minutes and keep it warm. Sprinkle the orange juice over the birds and dot with the remaining ounce of butter. Preheat the grill, then cook the poussins until golden and crisp. Add the grated orange rind, the Dijon and the cream to the sauce, let it bubble for a minute or so, check the seasoning, then pour around the chickens. Serve with plain boiled rice or new potatoes and some tiny green beans.

For a pudding try this method of baked apples.

Baked apples Bendigo

4 large Granny Smith apples
12 dates
2 oz of ginger in syrup

4 oz of soft brown sugar
6 fl oz sauternes or moselle
whipped cream

Core the apples and make a faint incision around the centre of each. Remove stones from dates and insert a thin slice of ginger instead. Stuff the apples with three dates each and the brown sugar. Put the apples into a gratin dish, pour the wine over them. Bake in a preheated oven at Gas 6, 400° F, 205° C for 45 minutes or until the apples are soft when pierced. Spoon the juices over the fruit, bring hot to the table and serve with great dollops of chilled whipped cream. This is really amazingly good. Enjoy.

7 May 1988

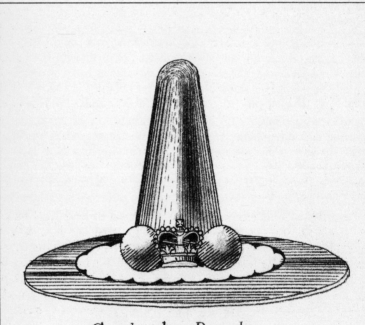

Cambridge Bomb.
Bombe à la Cambridge
serve with George's Cheltenham Wafers.

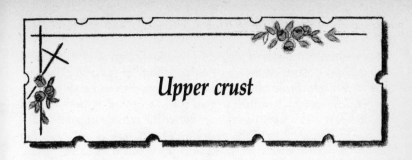

Upper crust

Another terrible Bank Holiday Monday when all thoughts of summery eating, salads and flummeries retreat in favour of good old casseroles or soup of a comforting nature. However, having been faced with a truly horrible Beef Wellington last week I thought you might like the following receipt, which is quite the best and most flavourful method I have ever encountered. It is an expensive dish but as a party piece it is impressive and there is no waste.

Beef Wellington (boeuf en croûte)

1 fillet of beef, trimmed and tied, about 12 inches long

The marinade:
4 tablespoons light olive oil
2 medium carrots sliced
2 medium onions sliced
2 sticks of celery sliced

a good pinch of thyme and sage, a bayleaf
4 cloves, 6 peppercorns, 1 teaspoon of salt
8 oz dry white vermouth
4 tablespoons of brandy

Heat the oil in a saucepan, add all the vegetables, herbs and spices, cover and cook gently until tender. Place the fillet in a long dish or casserole, sprinkle with the salt, cover with the vegetable mixture, then pour on the vermouth and brandy, cover and leave in a cool place or a refrigerator for 24 hours, turning and basting every few hours. Scrape off the marinade (but keep it) and pat the beef dry with paper towels. Rub the meat with oil and place in a roasting pan, cover with oiled foil and place in a preheated oven at Gas 7, 425° F, 218° C, and roast for 25 minutes, turning and basting at half-time. Remove from oven and cool for 30 minutes.

Trim and chop 2 lb of mushrooms into small pieces. Finely chop four or five shallots, then sauté them both in 2 oz of butter for about eight minutes mixing and turning the while, add 4 fluid oz of madeira, port or medium sherry, boil rapidly until all liquid has evaporated, stir in 4

117

tablespoons of some respectable pâté de foie, mix well and turn into a bowl and cover until needed.

For the pastry you need 15 oz of plain flour, 7 oz of chilled butter, 2 oz chilled Cookeen or the like, two teaspoons of salt and 6 fluid oz of chilled water. Blend all the ingredients together and chill for two hours before using. It is done in two parts: a cooked bottom case to hold the beef and a flaky pastry top. Butter the outside of a $12'' \times 3\frac{1}{4}''$ loaf tin. Roll three fifths of the pastry into a rectangle of $16'' \times 7''$, lay it over the upside-down tin, press into place and trim so the pastry forms a case of $1\frac{1}{2}$ inches deep. Prick all over with a fork and chill for half an hour. Bake in the middle of a preheated oven at Gas 7, 425° F, 220° C until light brown, 12 to 15 minutes. Cool for ten minutes on the tin, then carefully unmould. Roll remaining pastry into a $16'' \times 7''$ rectangle, spread bottom half with $1\frac{1}{2}$ oz of soft butter, fold in half to enclose butter. Repeat with another $1\frac{1}{2}$ oz butter and fold again. Roll into a rectangle, then fold in thirds like a business letter. Chill for two hours, then roll into another rectangle of $16'' \times 10''$. Place the baked bottom case on a buttered baking sheet, spread half the mushroom mixture on the bottom of the case. Remove string from the beef and place it on top of the mushrooms, then cover with the rest of them. Beat an egg with half a teaspoon of water and paint the sides of the case; lay pastry top over the meat letting it flop over about an inch on sides of case, press together and trim if necessary. Paint with the egg glaze. Make cross-hatch marks over the pastry and three vent holes three inches apart. Insert tiny foil funnels for escaping steam. Bake in the middle of a preheated oven at Gas 7, 425° F, 220° C for 20 minutes, then lower the heat to Gas 5, 380° F, 193° C for another 20 minutes. Let the whole thing rest in a warm place for at least 20 minutes before serving. Carve with a very sharp knife into $1\frac{1}{2}$ inch slices. Use the marinade for a sauce.

Simmer the marinade and a dessertspoon of mushroom ketchup with 16 fluid oz of beef stock and one tablespoon of tomato purée for an hour. When reduced to 16 oz again, strain, return to saucepan, and thicken with two dessertspoons of corn flour mixed with 3 oz of madeira, port or sherry. Simmer until shiny and thickened, season to taste. If you like you can add a cup of sauce béarnaise. Beat it in gradually off the heat or it will curdle.

I know this seems quite complicated but it's fun once you start and you can of course cheat by buying the pastry, half short, half flaky. Cold, Beef Wellington is excellent, ideal for a grand buffet or picnicking at Glyndebourne, say. Lucky old you.

4 June 1988

1, The Lily. 2. The Cactus. 3. The Fan. 4. The Pyramid. 5. The Sachet. 6. A Corner Fan. 7. The Boats. 8. The Cockscomb *(See Chapter LXVII)*

Summer is a-goin' out

'Ere we go again, rain, rain rain; the skies are dark and dismal, thunder and lightning rend the air, every paper has winning receipts for jolly summer picnics or dainty al fresco dinners in the garden, and what is worse, this is the week of our own *Spectator* party, which necessitates the use of the garden to contain our overflowing guests, and if it pours with rain we will be sunk, sodden and saddened. It is time for prayers and miracles from below and above respectively. We have just about managed it for over ten years so keep everything crossed.

On pleasanter subjects I went to supper with Willie Landels a couple of weeks ago to find his daughter Francesca doing the cooking – quite right and proper – but it was also inventive, light and fresh tasting, in fact a delicious risotto. Here it is.

Francesca's seafood risotto

1 large fresh crab
2 lb squid
½ lb shelled cockles (not horrors in vinegar)
1½ pints fish stock
1 fish head (cod or salmon)
2 oz freshly grated parmesan cheese

1 cup frozen petits pois
the grated rind of one lemon
1 large glass white wine
15 oz Italian risotto rice – Arborio
2 tablespoons olive oil
salt and pepper

Remove the flesh from the crab, retaining the white meat only for the risotto. (Use the dark meat for a lovely sandwich with lettuce and lemon juice.) Don't be frightened of dealing with the crab, just do it once and you will do it for life. Everything is edible except the bag-like stomach near the mouth, gills and grey-green lungs which look like felt. Use a rolling pin to crack the claws. Hit gently to avoid splintering. Clean the squid, removing heads, beaks and the transparent quill, rinse and cut into rings. Ask your fishmonger if nervous. Make the fish stock with the fish head and the crab shell, carrot, onion, bayleaf and peppercorns. Simmer in two pints of water for two hours, season, then strain. Pour the olive oil into a large saucepan, heat gently, then add the rice, stirring vigorously until thoroughly coated with the oil. Add the wine and the lemon rind then slowly add some of the stock, little by little, until the rice is fluid but not watery. After five to eight minutes, mix in the white crab meat, cook for a further three minutes then add the squid and lastly the cockles. Keep stirring all the time, making sure the rice does not stick to the bottom of the pan. Keep adding the stock so that the mixture becomes a thick fluid mass. Keep tasting the rice at minute intervals to ascertain how cooked it is, when nearly ready add the peas. When cooked, turn off the heat, stir in the parmesan cheese, check the seasoning, leave to stand for two minutes then serve immediately. The cooking of the rice should take about 20 minutes.

Here is a most marvellous pudding that I include with other miracles of the kitchen such as mayonnaise and beurre blanc. It seems to have no reason for working or setting but it does. I got the receipt from Fergus Provan of the Chanterelle years ago. I think it is called a pomfry, or is that a horse? Anyway it is a dream.

────── *Lemon and ratafia cream* ──────

1 pint of double cream
the juice of four lemons
the finely grated rind of three lemons

ratafia biscuits
6 oz of caster sugar or to taste

Bring the cream to simmering point in a good stainless steel saucepan but do not boil. When it is just simmering take off the heat and immediately add the grated lemon rind and sugar. Mix very well together then leave to get tepid. Pour in the lemon juice, blending all smoothly. Put enough ratafias to cover the bottom of a pretty dish or if you prefer use individual little ramekins or the like. Pour the lemon cream over the biscuits which will float up to the top. Set in the refrigerator for at least six hours or overnight. What could be simpler? Serve with some more ratafias on the side and, if you wish, some summer berries as an accompaniment.

9 July 1988

Colour delights

When visiting the sick in hospital or other places I tend to take food rather than flowers or fruit, both of which will be there in abundance anyway. Something with a good strong taste like salami or a fine cheese livens up the diet a treat, and a jam jar full of proper vinaigrette helps the sad salad days. Earlier in the year poor Patrick Proctor had a terrible burst stomach ulcer. There he was, 'long, lean and lanky with nothing to eat', so I asked what he might possibly enjoy. Some asparagus mousse was his heart's desire. Here it is, and all the tastier for being tinned asparagus, with its stronger flavour.

Asparagus mousse

8 hard-boiled eggs
1 pint of aspic
2 tins of asparagus (15 oz approx. each)

$\frac{1}{2}$ pint of double cream
salt and pepper
white wine and lemon juice

Buy the cut bits and tips of asparagus rather than the whole ones, they are cheaper but just as good. Drain the juice from them into a pint measuring jug. If not quite a pint, top up with water or white wine and a touch of lemon juice, and use this to make the aspic. Chop the hard-boiled eggs into fairly small pieces. Put the asparagus into a large bowl and mash with a fork. Whip the cream until it is slightly thickened and leaves a trail when dripping off the beater. Combine the cooled aspic with the eggs and the asparagus, then fold in the cream, season with fresh ground pepper and salt to taste, and maybe a touch more lemon juice. Pour into a soufflé dish or little bowls for travelling. Chill well until set. Serve from the dish, or you can turn it out and surround with cherry tomatoes, olives or what you will for prettiness.

From the pale green of the above receipt we go to the brilliant red of beetroots. I had a splendid Sunday lunch last week with the Scoones family. Francesca is an excellent cook with a helpful husband. We were having roast, glazed pork and she served these wonderful spiced beetroots with it, an absolutely stunning combination.

——— Gingered beetroots ———

1½ lbs of boiled beetroot
fresh ginger root
1 teaspoon of ground ginger
2 teaspoons of cornflour

2 fluid oz of cider vinegar
the juice and rind of an orange
4 oz soft brown sugar
3 oz of butter

If you can find tiny beetroots get them, but any will do. You will just have to chop the larger ones into chunks. Grate the rind off the orange, and chop finely about an inch of fresh ginger. In a saucepan large enough to contain everything, place the sugar, ground ginger, cornflour, fresh ginger and orange rind and mix to a paste with the vinegar and the orange juice. Bring slowly to the boil then simmer for a minute or two until thickened and shiny. Add the butter in small pieces, stirring the while. Mix in the beetroot and cook until heated through. Check for seasoning, sprinkle with chopped parsley or coriander and serve; perfectly delicious.

If, horrified by the terrible tales of travelling abroad, you have decided to go to some nice British resort for the hols, I suggest you take a splendid new Penguin book with you both for reading and experimentation. It is *English Seafood Cookery* by Richard Stein. He has a seafood restaurant in Padstow, Cornwall and deals with every fish and mollusc in our waters. He has some very exciting hors d'oeuvres including hot kipper salad with whisky or anchovy ice cream in puff pastry, but here is:

——— [Hake and potato pie] ———
(with a garlic, parsley and breadcrumb crust)

1 lb of peeled potatoes
4 oz of butter
1 lb of skinned hake fillet

2 slices of good white bread
2 cloves of garlic
salt, pepper and parsley

Set your oven to Gas 6, 400° F, 200° C. Cut the potatoes into ¼ inch slices. Cook for two minutes in boiling salted water. Smear half the butter round an oven dish. In the dish place the drained potatoes and the hake cut into one inch slices. Season, and dot the rest of the butter on top. Cover the dish and bake for 15 minutes, basting twice. Put the bread, garlic and parsley with a little salt and pepper in a food processor and reduce to crumbs. Cover the fish and potatoes with the crumbs and bake uncovered for a further five minutes or until crisp.

August 1988

Shrunk shanks and sweetiepie

With any luck this Monday is the last bogus Bank Holiday of the year; I'm glad the Notting Hill Carnival ended without too much bloodshed or troubles so that everyone could return to their homes in peace. I put up a cousin for the night as she couldn't get back to her flat since there were too many police cordons. Hey-ho, what a merry fiesta. Why don't they hold it just before Lent commences as all other countries do? All that good fried chicken would be very comforting on a chilly February day. I have made a new discovery in comfort food — sheep's shanks. Now that so many butchers prepare ready assembled kebabs, the leftover shank is readily available. If you enjoy glutinous meat like the knuckle end of a leg of lamb, oxtail, osso bucco and the like, you will love these shanks. One for each person should be enough.

——— *Lamb shanks* ———

6 lamb shanks
$\frac{1}{2}$ pint dry white wine
$\frac{1}{2}$ pint beef stock
3 oz unsalted butter
1 tablespoon sunflower oil
3 garlic cloves

$\frac{1}{2}$ lb onions
$\frac{1}{2}$ lb carrots
bouquet garni of bay leaf and
   rosemary
plain flour, salt and pepper

Put about 2 oz of flour, salt and freshly ground pepper into a plastic bag, toss the shanks one by one in the bag and lay them out on some greaseproof paper. Peel and chop the vegetables into chunks, slice the garlic finely. Place half the butter and oil in a large frying pan; when hot, brown the shanks in relays, keeping them at the ready. In a large casserole heat the rest of the butter and oil then add the vegetables and garlic, cook slowly until slightly browned, pour in the wine, bring to simmering and reduce for about five minutes. Pile in the lamb shanks, add the stock and the bouquet garni. Cover and either simmer on top of the stove or in a low oven for $1\frac{1}{2}$ hours until the meat is just falling off the bones. When cool enough, remove the meat from the bones, discarding the rather unsightly skin if you like. Or you can give each person a bone and a helping of the sauce and vegetables and let them fend for themselves. Check the seasoning before serving. Have a lovely mound of mashed potatoes to go with it and a green salad on the side. This meat if removed from the bone is very good eaten with the salsa verde served with the Italian bollito: oil, lemon juice, parsley, capers, garlic, salt and pepper, all mixed together as for vinaigrette.

Another method is to heat gently with chopped tinned tomatoes and a teaspoon of paprika. When hot, stir in four tablespoons of sour cream and serve with plain boiled potatoes.

Now for the Hungry Monk's famous pudding (plenty for eight).

——— *Banoffi pie* ———

12 oz uncooked shortcrust pastry	$\frac{3}{4}$ pint double cream
$1\frac{1}{2}$ tins of condensed milk ($13\frac{1}{2}$oz size)	$\frac{1}{2}$ teaspoon powdered instant coffee
$1\frac{1}{2}$ lb of firm bananas	1 dessertspoon caster sugar
	freshly ground coffee

The secret of this amazing pudding lies in the condensed milk which you must immerse unopened in a deep pan of boiling water. Cover and boil for five hours! It is vital to top up the pan of boiling water frequently, otherwise the tins will explode, causing grave risk to life, limb and kitchen ceilings. When cooked remove from the pan and cool completely before opening. Inside you will find the soft toffee filling. Preheat the oven to Gas 5, 380° F, 193° C. Lightly grease a 10″ flan tin. Line this with the pastry thinly rolled out. Prick the base all over with a fork, bake blind until crisp (20–25 minutes). Cool. Whip the cream with the instant coffee and sugar until thick and smooth. Spread the condensed milk toffee over the base of the flan. Peel and halve the bananas lengthways and lay them on the toffee. Finally spoon the cream all over the top and sprinkle with the fresh ground coffee. Serve in thick slices to the joy of the consumers both young and old. The great thing about this pudding is that it can be assembled in a trice once you have the toffee ready. If you boil several tins of condensed milk at the same time they will keep unopened indefinitely. Please, *please* do not make this pudding if you are absent-minded – think of the explosion.

3 September 1988

Milky ways and Chinese chook

I received a nice letter from a worried Mrs Margaret Hankins from Oswestry, who was concerned about all those tins of condensed milk exploding throughout the country when being boiled for Banoffi Pie (3 September). She offers an alternative method for the caramel filling, with 4 oz margarine, 4 oz brown sugar, 2 tablespoons of golden syrup and a small tin of condensed milk. Heat the ingredients gently until melted, bring to the boil and simmer for eight minutes. Beat well with a wooden spoon as it cools until smooth and beginning to thicken. Use at will. It must be even sweeter than the other. However, many thanks.

Now that pork has gone the way of all flesh and is being produced without enough fat to make good crackling (I think they put water in instead – it seems to exude from every pore) I found the following receipt in a very good book, *The Cooking of South-West France* by Paula Wolfert. The pork, being cooked in milk, gets back a little butterfat and the meat keeps moist and juicy.

3½ to 4 lbs pork loin, boned and rolled and well trimmed

2 plump cloves of garlic, cut into slivers

coarse salt

1 small carrot, finely chopped

1 small onion, finely chopped

the white part of a small leek, finely sliced

1 oz of unsalted butter

1½ pints of creamy milk

¼ teaspoon of ground white pepper

bouquet garni of parsley, thyme and bayleaf

tablespoon of chopped parsley

Two days before cooking, stud the meat with the garlic slivers, rub the surface with coarse salt, cover loosely and keep refrigerated. Preheat the oven to Gas 2, 300° F, 150° C. In a large, deep, flameproof casserole slowly fry the vegetables until soft but not brown. Place the pork on top of the vegetables and keep on a low heat. Bring the milk to boiling point in a saucepan, then pour round the pork. Add the bouquet garni and sprinkle with the pepper. Cover and place on the lowest rack in the oven for three hours, turning the meat at intervals.

Remove the casserole and raise the oven temperature to Gas 5, 375° F, 190° C. Transfer the meat to an open baking dish, fat side up, and return to the oven to brown for 20 minutes. Meanwhile, strain the cooking juices into a narrow deep container such as a measuring jug, pushing down on the milk solids that have separated in the cooking. Chill quickly (in the freezer or surrounded by ice cubes) so that the fat rises to the surface and can be removed. Return the cooking liquid to the casserole and bring to the boil with a metal spoon on the bottom to prevent the liquid boiling over (good trick). Reduce by two thirds (takes about 15 minutes). Adjust seasoning to taste.

Slice the meat and arrange in overlapping slices on a fine serving platter. Spoon the sauce all over the meat and sprinkle with parsley. Serve the pork surrounded with lovely little glacé vegetables; onions, carrots and turnips. Any leftover pork is excellent served cold with a salad.

Here is something I do with chicken pieces which gives them a good flavour, sort of fake Chinese. Use whichever bits you prefer; I like the thighs.

8 chicken thighs
2 tablespoons soy sauce
3 tablespons dry sherry
2 garlic cloves, finely chopped
one-inch chunk of fresh ginger, peeled
   and chopped

teaspoon of dried tarragon
juice of half a lemon
chicken stock

Remove any excess lumps of fat. Place the chicken pieces in a cooking dish that can receive them in one layer. Add the soy sauce, sherry, garlic, ginger, tarragon and lemon juice. Marinate for a couple of hours, giving them the odd turn. When ready to cook, let the skin be uppermost. Top up the marinade with chicken stock to cover the flesh but not the skin. Preheat the oven to Gas 6, 400° F, 205° C. Cook for 30–35 minutes, or until done, remove from the oven, grind some salt and pepper over the skin and finish off under a hot grill to make them really crisp. Serve with a good dish of rice and whatever vegetable tickles your fancy.

1 October 1988

Clocks back

Once we have turned the clocks back I feel we have had it for a long duration; those terrible early evenings fill me with gloom, it's dark in the morning whatever they do, so why ruin the afternoon as well? There is talk of it being abolished (Greenwich Mean Time) and aligning Britain permanently with European time which should have been done years ago if the farmers, north Scotland and the construction industry hadn't put the kybosh on it. Roll on time change, quicker the better.

Paradoxically the weather seems better than the summer which ain't difficult and the market is full of good and cheaper vegetables. The aubergines were looking especially shiny and plump so I thought to cook them in the Catalan way which I had forgotten about until having them in Penrith this summer dished up by the ravishing Annie Liddel.

──────── *Aubergines en gigot* ────────

You must get the amount of aubergines you want making sure they are very shiny, plump and unblemished; when dull and getting wrinkly they are nearly always dry and discoloured inside.

What you are meant to do is to make two rows of little incisions into each whole, unpeeled aubergine, then insert tiny strips of smoked bacon and slithers of garlic which have been rolled in fresh ground salt and pepper and marjoram into alternate incisions. I find this operation devilish tricky so instead I cut two whole-length incisions at 20 past and 20 to and stuff them with the herbed bacon and garlic. Place them in a casserole, pour some good olive oil over them with a sprinkling of salt and pepper, cover the dish and bake in a slow oven for about an hour or until well cooked through. Pierced with a skewer, they should be totally soft. Serve as a first course or a savoury. They are excellent cold, sliced open, and salted with some fresh oil trickled over them.

Frances Bissell has done it again, she has written another very good cookbook which would be ideal for Digby Anderson's poor Gavin of 15th October when he has progressed from his pasta cooking. *Ten Dinner Parties for Two* by Frances Bissell (Ebury Press, £8.95) is a collection of treats and easy meals from her home dinners with her husband and very delicious and original they are too. I have just cooked my first oxtail this season; I do it with Guinness, this is Frances's method with wine.

──────── *Oxtail stew for two* ────────

1 generous lb of oxtail	$\frac{1}{2}$ teaspoon of chestnut or potato flour
1 small onion, sliced	1 teaspoon of blueberry, bilberry or
2 garlic cloves, crushed	cherry jam
5 fluid oz of good red wine	2 teaspoons of malt whisky or kirsh
$\frac{1}{3}$ teaspoon dill weed	salt and freshly ground pepper

Trim as much fat as possible from the chunks of oxtail and fry until well browned in a nonstick frying pan. (If you haven't got one use a little oil in a good heavy pan). Transfer to a casserole. Fry the onion in the frying pan until just browning, add the garlic and fry together for 30 seconds. Pour on the wine and add the dill seed, cook for another

30 seconds then pour over the oxtail. Cover and barely simmer for 2 hours.

Remove the oxtail from the sauce. Cool it rapidly, cover and refrigerate overnight. Do the same with the sauce, sieving it first.

Next day separate the meat from the bone and scrape the fat from the top of the sauce. Place the meat and the sauce in a pan and heat slowly. Mix the flour with a little water and stir into the stew. When it has thickened slightly add the jam then season to taste. About five minutes before serving pour in the spirit; the alcohol will have evaporated by the time you serve the dish. Tiny new potatoes go well with the stew, also broccoli florets and thinly sliced carrots which have both been steamed for 5 minutes only.

Another original first course and a delight to the eye is:

———— *Quail's eggs baked in new potatoes* ————

6 small new potatoes (2 oz each)
6 quail's eggs
1 oz unsalted butter

Scrub the potatoes, scoop out a hollow in each potato with a melon baller, large end. Remove a very thin slice from each bottom to allow it to stand steady. Boil the potatoes until *just* cooked. Drain. Brush the potatoes inside and out with melted butter, season lightly and stand on an oiled baking tray. Crack an egg into each potato. Bake in the top half of a preheated oven at Gas 4, 350° F, 180° C for 8 to 10 minutes, serve immediately.

17 November 1988

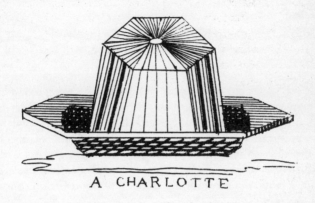

A CHARLOTTE

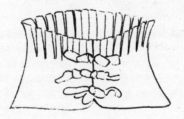

Mould for Buns

Feast days

Advent comes but once a year, but it seems to come round increasingly quickly. Those terrible switching on the lights ceremonies always give a sense of dread. Nevertheless, Advent is meant to be a time of preparation for the coming of the Christ Child and also for the festivities that go with it, so I thought you might make a Christmas cake this week. This is the best cake I have ever tasted, made by the wonderful lady who cares for my uncle, the 'Good Canon'. She is also a wild voyager.

———— Rich Christmas cake ————

18 oz currants
8 oz each sultanas and stoned raisins
4 oz mixed peel
6 oz glacé cherries, halved
10 oz plain flour and a pinch of salt
$\frac{1}{2}$ level teaspoon each, mixed spice and cinnamon
10 oz butter

10 oz soft brown sugar
the grated rind of $\frac{1}{2}$ a lemon
6 well-beaten eggs
3 oz ground almonds
3 tablespoons brandy
1 tablespoon black treacle
2 tablespoons milk

Line a nine-inch cake tin with two layers of greaseproof paper and tie a double band of good brown paper around the outside of it. Mix all the fruit with the flour, salt and spices. Cream the butter with the sugar and lemon rind until soft and creamy, the mixture should drop from the spoon with ease. Add the eggs little by little, beating well each time. Fold in half the flour and fruit until well amalgamated then fold in the other half together with the grated almonds and treacle and finally the brandy and milk. Pour into the cake tin, spreading evenly but making a slight dip in the centre. Preheat the oven to Gas $1\frac{1}{2}$, 300° F, 149° C. Stand the tin on a layer of newspaper just below the centre of the oven and bake for 5 to $5\frac{1}{4}$ hours. After $2\frac{1}{2}$ hours of the cooking time cover the top of the tin with about four layers of grease-proof paper to prevent over browning. Start testing at five hours with a skewer, which should come out clean after piercing the cake. When cooked, cool the cake in its tin on a rack then turn out. Before storing in a good airtight tin pierce the cake with a skewer or knitting needle in several places and drip a further 3 tablespoons of brandy into it with the aid of an eye dropper or what you will.

Bonbons are another good thing to have around. Truffles are easy enough to make and half the cost of bought ones, which are quite often stale. Here are the irresistible ones à la Rubinstein.

———— Fresh cream truffles ————

$\frac{1}{2}$ pint thick double cream
1 vanilla pod
1 egg yolk
1 oz caster sugar
5 oz best plain chocolate (Menier)
1 oz unsalted butter

1 tablespoon brandy, rum or Tia Maria or any liqueur or 1 teaspoon instant coffee powder
4 oz plain chocolate for coating
pure cocoa powder
1 teaspoon of tasteless salad oil

Bring the cream to the boil with the split vanilla pod. Remove from the heat, cover and leave to infuse. Whisk the egg yolk (praying against salmonella) with the sugar until pale and thick. Whisk into the cream and return to the heat very briefly to heat through, but be very careful not to boil. Keep whisking or you may scramble. Remove from the heat and fish out the vanilla pod. Stir in the first five oz of chocolate, broken into pieces, until melted and well blended. Place in the refrigerator for about half an hour until set but not hard. Using an electric or hand rotary beater whisk the softened butter and whichever flavouring you fancy into the chocolate cream mixture. Put the mixture into a piping bag with a half-inch nozzle and pipe little sausage shapes or balls onto a plate or a tray covered in foil. If you don't have a piping bag do your best with teaspoons. Replace in refrigerator until set quite hard, about an hour and a half minimum. Sift onto a plate enough cocoa powder to coat the truffles. Melt the remaining chocolate with the salad oil in a little bowl set over hot water or a proper bain marie if available; let it cool a little. Using a fine two-pronged fork or two tooth-picks, dip each truffle into the melted chocolate, coat on all sides then roll immediately in the cocoa. Refrigerate until wanted. Sooner the better, but will keep for up to three days.

3 December 1988

In for a duck

Thank heaven all that festive confusion is at last done with and we can continue in our usual modes of life without wondering which day of the week it is. We have about a month to go before a very early Lent this year, Ash Wednesday falling on 8 February, so let us indulge in the delicious but relatively expensive duck. Duck meat is a versatile viand, but a large duck will only be sufficient for four people.

I recently roasted a five-and-a-half pounder on a grid, having poured a kettle of boiling water over it for maximum crispness, then pierced it all over with fork prongs and rubbed in some salt, and the resulting fat from the bottom of the pan was 12 ounces in weight. Not that the fat isn't wonderful for frying, but you can't just eat it. Those clever Chinese invented the most economical way to eat duck, the Peking method, in which every scrap of the flesh is wrapped into a parcel.

Peking duck

1 duckling, about 5 lbs
2 tablespoons clear honey
16 spring onions

1 cucumber
Hoisin or plum sauce
Chinese pancakes

Remove giblets and liver from the duck's cavity (reserve giblets for stock, but use the liver for an omelette or a savoury on toast) and re-weigh. Place the bird in the sink and pour a kettle of boiling water over it, turning it to scald both sides. Dry inside and out with a cloth or paper towels. Loop a string under the wings, tie securely and hang in a cool draughty place for eight hours. (A north wind is preferred by the Chinese I believe.) Place the duck breast side up on a grid in a roasting tin with some water in the bottom. Paint the bird with the honey, then roast in a preheated oven Gas 6, 400 °F, 200 °C, without basting (15–20 minutes per pound), until the skin is dark and crisp. If you think it is getting over browned lower the heat to Gas 5, 375 °F,

190 °C. Allow to rest for about ten minutes before carving into little slices. The Chinese pancakes have been made previously, and you just steam them for ten minutes while the duck is resting.

———— Chinese pancakes (doilies) ————

1 lb plain white flour
12 fluid oz boiling water

1 tablespoon cold water
sesame oil

Sift the flour into a bowl. Gradually pour in the boiling water, beating quickly until well mixed, then stir in the cold water. Leave to cool then knead into a smooth dough; cover the bowl with a damp cloth and leave for half an hour. Place dough on a lightly floured board, divide into three portions, knead each until smooth. Roll each portion into a long roll and cut each one into ten discs. Roll the discs into balls then flatten them with the heel of your palm into circles of $2\frac{1}{2}$ inches. Brush half the pancakes (15) with sesame oil then cover each with one of the remaining pancakes. Roll each pair into a six-inch circle. Heat an unoiled heavy frying pan over a medium heat. Cook each double pancake for one or two minutes until it puffs up and develops brownish spots underneath, turn over and cook other side. Remove from pan and peel the two layers apart, stack on a plate and cover with a cloth until steamed. Cut the spring onions into two-inch strips and sliced length-wise. Slice the cucumber into matchstick size. Each person smears the pancake with sauce, fills it with some duck meat and skin, and some of the onion and cucumber. Roll up and tuck one end in to make a little purse. Great fun for children's parties; just what they like.

If you prefer plain roast duck, roast it as above, omitting the honey and the hanging in a north wind. Serve it with two sauces, old fashioned apple sauce for its tartness and sauce bigarade (bitter orange) for its sheer delight. Seville oranges should be just coming in so seize the chance. Pare the rind off two Seville oranges thinly with no pith, cut into tiny strips. Fling into boiling water for five minutes, strain. Melt 1 oz of butter in a little saucepan, stir in a level tablespoon of plain flour, cooking gently until pale coffee coloured, add about $\frac{1}{2}$ a pint of stock from the giblets a little at a time, simmer for a further 15 minutes, add the rind, two teaspoons of sugar, salt and pepper, the juice of one orange plus a slurp of madeira or port and finally any juices from the roasting pan after you have drained off the fat into a bowl. If you can't find Seville oranges use an ordinary one and a piled tablespoon of bitter marmalade, but omit the sugar.

14 January 1989

Chinese Lenten

What a lot of occasions at the beginning of February this year give thought for food rather than vice versa; Shrove Tuesday feasting, Ash Wednesday fasting, the Chinese New Year of the Snake for processing and Saint Valentine's day for loving and massacring. So with any luck most people all over the world should have a chance at one of these celebrations.

Inadvertently I made a rather good Lenten dish last week trying to finish off some leftover leeks and staling cream. If you are starting from scratch the following ingredients are what you need, but they could easily be interchangeable with your own leftovers.

Leek and tuna soufflé

1 lb trimmed leeks	¼ lb of goat's cheese (soft)
2 oz butter	pepper and salt
1 tablespoon plain flour	fresh grated parmesan
3 eggs	1 tin of tuna fish (7 oz)
¼ pint of thick cream	

Slice the cleaned leeks rather finely. Using a saucepan large enough for all the other items, stew the leeks in the butter until soft. Stir in the flour, mixing well. Continue cooking and stirring for three minutes, add the cream and then the goat's cheese, blending into a smooth mass. Season with a goodly grinding of black pepper and salt to taste. Remove from heat to cool down a bit. Separate the eggs, then add the yolks to the leek mixture one at a time, beating well. Butter a gratin dish or some suitable oven-proof receptacle about 12 inches long, scatter the drained tuna fish over the base. Now beat the whites of the eggs stiffly and fold them gently into the leeks. Pour onto the tuna and strew the top with some parmesan cheese. Place in a preheated oven at Gas 8, 445 °F, 229 °C, for 20 to 25 minutes. I happened to have two aging egg whites lurking in the refrigerator which I added to the other whites, thus aiding the rising of the soufflé, but that is not necessary. It makes a very good supper dish and goes well with a tomato salad.

Pork spare ribs are really expensive if you think of the small amount of meat you actually get off them, so for the following dish I substituted turkey wings, much cheaper and meatier. Cooked the same way as spare ribs they make an excellent vehicle for the sauce.

———— Red-cooked turkey wings ————

2–2½ lb turkey wings
1 large onion
paprika
1½ inch fresh ginger
2 tablespoons sherry

2 tablespoons soy sauce
2 tablespoons mushroom ketchup
¾ pint of good chicken stock
4 oz of pineapple (optional)
vegetable oil

Boil the turkey wings in a saucepan for ten minutes. Drain. Cut the wing tips off at the joint for easier handling. Return to a large pan. Chop the onion, grate the peeled ginger, add them to the wings; sprinkle with about a teaspoon of paprika and some ground black pepper, add the soy, sherry and mushroom ketchup, the chicken stock and if so desired the pineapple (this will achieve a sweet and sour flavour). Cover the pan (I used a large iron casserole) and simmer for threequarters of an hour, turning the wings every now and then to ensure even cooking. Remove the wings into a roasting pan. If the sauce is still rather liquid turn up the heat to reduce until you have a nice sticky covering sauce. Brush the wings with sunflower oil and coat with sauce. Place in a preheated oven at Gas 6, 400 °F, 205 °C and roast for 15 minutes. Serve as a first course to be eaten with the fingers or as a main one with plain boiled rice and some crispish green vegetable like mangetout or broccoli.

With all this talk of kidneys, I prepared a delicious little dish of lambs' kidneys the other day. Remove skin from eight kidneys, cut in half and cut out the white suet from inside. Sprinkle with salt and pepper on the insides, leave for half an hour. Gently sauté the kidneys in butter, making sure they remain just pink within, sprinkle with about two tablespoons of warmed Ricard or Pernod. When bubbling set fire to the juices and when flames die stir a quarter pint of thick cream until bubbling again. Serve at once on toast or with mashed potatoes. If you hate the Pernod taste use port instead.

11 February 1989

Rejoice – it's pink

L ast week we had Laetare Sunday, a joyful day in the middle of Lent when you can break your Lenten resolutions with impunity, eat drink and have a jolly time. The priests are vested in pink and the Pope blesses the Golden Rose. Mothering Sunday is said to derive from the pre-Reformation custom of visiting the 'Mother Church' on that day, and children in service normally returned to their homes with a small gift for their mother. I thought it would be appropriate to construct a pink lunch for this or another joyous occasion. We shall start with:

—— Salmon mousse ——

$1\frac{1}{2}$ lb fresh, cooked salmon, boned and
   skinned
$\frac{1}{4}$ lb softened butter
white of an egg
$\frac{1}{2}$ pint double cream

$1\frac{1}{2}$ level 5ml teaspoon of gelatine
2 tablespoons lemon juice
$\frac{1}{2}$ pint aspic made with white wine
   and water, $\frac{1}{2}$ & $\frac{1}{2}$
salt and pepper

Put the gelatine to soak in the lemon juice in a small bowl until spongy, then let it dissolve over hot water. Place the salmon in a food processor or blender, whizz until puréed, add the butter and whizz again. Stir in the white of egg, whizz once more. Pour this mixture into a chilled bowl sitting in a larger bowl with ice cubes at the bottom. Beat well with a wooden spoon until light and fluffy. Whip the cream to the soft peak stage. Add the dissolved gelatine, mixing thoroughly, then fold in the cream, season to taste. Pour half the aspic into a mould (a fish-shaped one if you have such a thing). Let it set in the refrigerator. Pack the mousse into the mould and cover with the rest of the aspic, chill for six hours until firm. Turn out onto a large plate, sprinkle with parsley and surround with lemon wedges. Serve with a rémoulade or a ravigote sauce.

A dainty chicken dish to follow, very suitable for mother, I hope; the combination of prawns and fowl producing an interesting flavour.

Pink poulet and prawns

1 medium chicken ($3\frac{1}{2}$–4 lbs)
8 fluid oz dry white wine
8 fluid oz water
about 36 prawns cooked in their
   shells

$\frac{1}{2}$ pint sour cream
2 teaspoons tomato purée
1 level tablespoon cornflour.

Peel the prawns, reserving their heads and shells. Bone the chicken and remove all skin. Cut the meat into generous pieces and season with salt and fresh ground pepper. (You may prefer to buy chicken pieces to the equivalent of a whole bird.) Place the flesh, leg meat first, into a bowl that will fit into a saucepan for steaming. Put the bowl into the saucepan containing the wine, water and the prawn heads and shells, cover tightly and simmer gently for an hour until the flesh is cooked. Remove the chicken from the bowl into a suitable serving dish, mix with the peeled prawns and keep warm. Strain the liquid from the saucepan into a smaller pan and add any juice left in the chicken's bowl. Bring to the boil and reduce to a syrup consistency. Check the seasoning then pour over the chicken and prawns. Put the sour cream and tomato purée into the pan, heat gently mixing the whole until just bubbling then add the cornflour dissolved in a little white wine to thicken, cook for a minute or two then stir into the chicken dish. Serve with plain boiled rice and bright green peas or beans.

For pudding we need something fresh and fruity after those two cream-laden courses. This can be done well beforehand, but try not to chill it.

Nectarines with raspberry syrup

6 large nectarines
8 oz granulated sugar

1 lb of raspberries, fresh or frozen
2 tablespoons of kirsch

Wash the nectarines then poach them in a pint of boiling water for four minutes. Remove the fruit from the water with a slotted spoon onto a cloth. Peel them carefully and return the skins to the poaching water. Place the nectarines in a beautiful glass bowl. Add the sugar and the raspberries to the water, bring to the boil and cook rapidly for ten minutes. Strain the syrup through a sieve lined with butter-muslin into another saucepan. Cook the strained syrup for another five minutes until it has thickened and reduced slightly. Take off the heat and allow to get lukewarm, add the kirsch (or any suitable liqueur you may have) and pour over the nectarines. Exit mother crying happily.

11 March 1989

Birthday treats

I thought we had lost the feast of the Annunciation on 25 March and would have to cancel Christmas, but I find it was retrieved and put on my birthday, which is a great treat. I have never had a grand feast just popped in for convenience before, though I have alighted on Easter just by luck. I suppose old Durham would rather think of the Annunciation as a telephone call, to modernise the event, but I have always loved this feast and all the wonderful paintings it has inspired, specially when there is a direct line from the Holy Ghost to the Blessed Virgin's ear. I haven't done much for cakes and I have never been fond of the white and pink or blue variety. I always had a great coffee cake for my childhood birthdays but the following is dark, dangerous and delicious:

──────── *Devil's food cake* ────────

$\frac{1}{4}$ lb butter
$\frac{1}{4}$ lb golden syrup
2 oz soft brown sugar
$\frac{1}{4}$ lb chocolate Menier
$\frac{1}{2}$ teaspoon of bicarbonate of soda

4 tablespoons milk
$\frac{1}{2}$ lb self-raising flour
small pinch of salt
1 large egg

You need two eight-inch sandwich tins. Grease them and line the bottom with baking paper. Heat the oven to Gas 3, 325 °F, 163 °C. Melt the butter, syrup, sugar and chocolate in a saucepan, stirring regularly until smooth, but do not allow to boil. Cool. Dissolve the bicarbonate of soda in one tablespoon of the milk in a little cup. Sieve the flour and

140

salt into a mixing-bowl and make a well in the centre. Beat in the treacle mixture, remaining milk and the egg, using a wooden spoon, then mix in the bicarbonate of soda. Divide equally into the two tins. Bake in the middle of the oven for 35 minutes. Turn out onto racks and leave to cool, removing the paper linings. Make a butter icing using 2 oz unsalted butter, $\frac{1}{4}$ lb of icing sugar and six drops of vanilla essence (not flavouring). Beat the butter with a wooden spoon until soft and creamy, then gradually beat in the icing sugar until it has all been used up; add the vanilla drops, mixing very well. Sandwich the cakes together with the icing. Now for the top icing, which is American frosting. You need $\frac{1}{2}$ lb granulated sugar, 4 tablespoons water, 1 egg white and 1 further oz chocolate Menier, and a sugar thermometer if you happen to possess one. Put the sugar and water into a good heavy based saucepan, heat gently until dissolved. Bring to the boil and continue boiling without stirring until the syrup reaches the temperature of 240 °F. (If you have no thermometer the syrup is ready when a small drop forms a soft ball when put into cold water.) Whisk the egg white into soft peaks in a bowl large enough to accommodate the syrup. Whisking the while, pour the syrup into the egg-white and continue whisking until the icing thickens and has a slightly granular feel. Pour over the top of the cake and smooth quickly with a stainless knife dipped in hot water. Sprinkle with grated chocolate just before the icing sets. It looks beautiful.

Another good party piece and a good way of using up a ham end is:

───── *Hot ham mousse with spinach* ─────

1 lb cooked ham
2 egg whites
16 oz thick cream, chilled

spinach
salt and pepper

Chop the ham roughly and put it in a food processor with the egg whites, season with salt and freshly ground pepper, whizz until it becomes a paste. Turn out into a bowl and gradually stir in the cream. Grease a ring mould of suitable size with butter and pour in the mousse. Set the mould in a baking-tin with hot water coming an inch or two up the side of the mould and bake in a pre-heated oven at Gas 3, 350 °F, 177 °C for about 45 minutes, or until the mousse is firm. Remove mould from the hot water and leave to settle for a few minutes on a rack. Turn out onto a fine dish and fill the well in the middle with fresh cooked spinach seasoned with nutmeg and salt. Surround the mousse with triangles of crisp fried croutons and serve with a velouté sauce mixed with mushrooms. Use a light chicken stock for the sauce, which is made like a bechamel, but using stock instead of milk, and should be cooked for about an hour, seasoned well with the addition of $\frac{1}{2}$ lb of sliced mushrooms once it has started to simmer.

8 April 1989

Nuts in May

With a hey nonny nonny and a hotchacha, what a jolly little May Day festival we had. Rioting in six countries, prisoners on the tiles and general gloom abounding; it always works. But there was a much greater and far more enjoyable Russian feast going on the day before, namely Easter, which the Eastern Church still celebrates independently according to the old calendar. There is always a feast after the deprivations of Lent and the traditional dessert is a great, glorious creamy pyramid called Paskha. I have rooted around among my friends with Russian connections and have come up with the following:

——— Paskha ———

12 oz fresh curd cheese or cream
    cheese unsalted
5 oz sour cream or crème fraîche
$\frac{1}{2}$ lb unsalted butter
$\frac{1}{2}$ lb caster sugar

4 egg yolks
vanilla essence (not flavouring)
1 lb mixed, chopped almonds,
    sultanas, glacé cherries, pineapple
    and angelica

Press the cheese through the finest sieve of a mouli or similar. Cream the butter, sugar and egg yolks together until the sugar has dissolved.

Mix in the sour cream and the vanilla essence to taste, about six to eight drops I reckon, then gradually stir in the cream cheese until thoroughly blended. Pour all the chopped fruits and nuts into the concoction and mix well. The Russians have special paskha moulds which are the traditional pyramid shape, but as most of us don't have one, use a colander lined with damp butter muslin or a clean, lined flower-pot of the earthenware variety with a hole in the bottom for the moisture of the cheese to escape. Put the mixture in one of these containers, cover with damp butter muslin, a plate and a 2 lb weight; leave in a cold place for 24 hours. When ready, unmould on to a dish, and if you really want to be traditional you can sculpt the pudding into a pyramid with a palette knife and stick a red rose on the top. The lovely Louise Patten says she leaves the paskha for 48 hours, letting the fruit flavours get stronger. They used to have an ex-lady-in-waiting to the Czarina living with them when they were children who didn't care for the dried fruit in the paskha so made it without. If you still have feelings about salmonella there is a cooked version:

——— *Cooked paskha* ———

2 lbs unsalted fresh curd or cream cheese	1 lb unsalted butter
	10 oz of sour cream
6 egg yolks	vanilla essence
1 lb caster sugar	$\frac{1}{2}$ lb chopped almonds

Wrap the cheese in a clean cloth and put it between two boards for 6–8 hours with a weight on top to get rid of the moisture. Cream the sugar, butter and egg yolks as above, mix in the sour cream and vanilla and finally the cheese (sieved again). Stir in the almonds. Put the mixture into a double saucepan, heat to simmering point but on no account boil. Let it cool, then proceed to mould as before.

I feel a soufflé would be suitable for Ascension day, and as the delicious little purple and white young turnips are in the market seize the chance.

8¼ inches long   2s 6d each
No.31 — ASPARAGUS

Young turnip soufflé

1 lb young turnips
2 fat cloves of garlic
2 oz butter
$1\frac{1}{2}$ oz plain flour
$\frac{1}{4}$ pint of the turnip cooking water
4 fluid oz milk

4 egg yolks
1 tablespoon chopped parsley
5 egg whites
1 tablespoon breadcrumbs (fine)
1 tablespoon fresh grated parmesan
   cheese
seasoning

Peel the turnips, chop in half and cook in boiling salted water with the garlic until just tender, strain well and purée. Melt the butter in a large saucepan, stir in the flour, cook for a minute, then add the turnip water and milk slurp by slurp until smooth. Add the turnips, remove from the heat and beat in the egg yolks one at a time. Season strongly and add the parsley. Whisk the egg whites until stiff, then gently fold into the turnip mixture. Have ready a well buttered $2\frac{1}{2}$ pint soufflé dish, sprinkle the cheese and crumbs round the sides and bottom, turning the dish so that the surfaces are evenly coated, tip the residue onto some paper. Spoon the soufflé into the dish and strew with the leftover cheese and crumbs. Preheat the oven to Gas 6, 400 °F, 200 °C, with a baking tray set in the middle. Place soufflé on tray and cook for 30 minutes. Do not peek.

6 May 1989

Modern Mould.

Boiled Pudding

Cold treats

We have now come to a lull after all the high days and holidays (both proper and improper) we have been enjoying, probably a lull in the amazing May weather as well; June has been very wet for years which is sad, as heavy rain tends to drown the little partridges, who are sorely taxed for shelter in this destructive age, but, who knows? We may continue fair, fruitful and frightfully hot. We did once upon a time.

I had a sea trout last week: what a fine fish, better than salmon, I think and it comes in more suitable sizes for the average meal. I had some left over, but not enough for a main course in itself, so I made this tomato ring, which, with the trout placed in the middle covered in leftover green mayonnaise, made an excellent and ravishing supper dish.

Bloody Mary aspic

1 litre (1¾ pints) tomato juice
4 tablespoons medium sherry or vodka
2 tablespoons lemon juice

celery salt
tabasco and Worcester sauce
1½ packets of aspic or gelatine (17g)
¼ pint single cream

You need a 2½ pint ring mould for this, but if you haven't got one handy, never mind, use a loaf tin or whatever; you will just have to put the leftovers around rather than in the centre. Pour about a quarter-pint of the tomato juice into a small saucepan, bring to the boil, then throw in the aspic or gelatine off the heat, stirring like mad until it is thoroughly dissolved. Never let it boil or it will self-destruct and not gel. When it is totally smooth pour it into the rest of the juice waiting in a jug or bowl. Season with the salt, about ten shakes of tabasco, Worcester sauce to taste (1 dessert spoon?), the lemon juice, sherry or vodka and mix thoroughly; check the taste is to your liking. Drizzle the cream into the mixture just giving it the odd swirl, then pour the lot into the mould, which has been rinsed out in cold water. Chill in the refrigerator until set, which is speeded up if the juice was already chilled. Turn out the mould on to a large plate, fill the middle with whatever you fancy (salmon, chicken, tuna, etc) and cover with mayonnaise. You could surround it with cold broad beans dressed with olive oil and lemon: a pretty sight indeed. I have said one-and-a half packets of aspic or gelatine as I found two full ones made it over-stiff, but if you prefer that effect use the two.

Ages ago I gave a receipt for a crab pâté and the other day I turned it into a lighter mousse which the recipients liked very much, so here it is.

———— *Crab mousse* ————

1lb crab meat, $\frac{1}{2}$ white, $\frac{1}{2}$ brown, fresh or frozen
4 large eggs
4 tablespoons freshly grated parmesan cheese
4 tablespoons thick cream
6 oz unsalted butter
3 tablespoons medium sherry
tabasco or cayenne pepper
lemon juice

Separate the egg yolks from the whites into two bowls. Mix the sherry and the cream into the yolks and beat well. Place the butter and the crab meat into a good saucepan, cook gently until melted and blended together, pour in the egg, cream and sherry, continue cooking over a gentle heat stirring all the time with a wooden spoon (we don't want scrambled eggs, so be careful, use a heat mat) until thickened, add the parmesan cheese, stirring again until melted. Season with the lemon juice and tabasco to suit your taste. Remove from the heat and leave to cool, giving it the odd stir. When cool, whip the egg whites stiffly, then gently fold into the crab. Spoon into a soufflé dish and chill for about six hours. Serve with some hot brown toast.

Ices, strictly speaking, are water ice including neither eggs nor milk, but a marquise is an ice enriched with whipped cream at the end and is very fresh-tasting and delicious. With any luck we should have a bumper crop of strawberries to play around with, so I thought this would be good to have up your sleeves.

———— *Marquise of strawberries* ————

Crush about four small punnets of strawberries and either put them through a fine sieve or liquidise if you don't mind the pips. Sweeten to taste and add enough cold water to make a pint of liquid. Boil 8 oz of granulated sugar in 15 oz of water for five minutes. Cool the syrup and stir into the strawberry purée, add the juice of a lemon. Freeze in a plastic box, beating every half-hour to prevent crystals. When ready to serve stir in a pint of whipped cream and 8 fluid oz of kirsch or any of the fruit liqueurs. Quite a treat.

3 June 1989

Midsummer matters

Some good feast days back again. As I write it is Midsummer Day, birthday of poor St John the Baptist; on 29 June it is SS Peter and Paul, a suitable day for eating the very delicious fish John Dory, otherwise known as St Peter's fish, with his finger marks left on each side. And we can toast St Paul with a new unit of wine for all our stomachs' sakes, though I'm sure he would have been furious, as usual, with a mere unit. We have just had SS John Fisher and Thomas More, so quite a few heads have been rolling. But enough of all that. The following receipt I have adapted from one given to me by the indomitable, great and good Anne Oxford. It was rather vague as to quantities and measurements, so I have tried it out and adapted it and hope you approve. It is a good summer party dish and extremely rich, I'm glad to say.

Chicken Demidoff

1 chicken of 3½–4lbs
8 oz chicken livers
½ pint thick cream
1 packet gelatine, ¼ oz
medium sherry or the like (vermouth, madeira)
2 carrots

2 onions
parsley stalks, bay leaf, thyme, tarragon
1 clove garlic
3 oz unsalted butter
lemon, salt and pepper

Rub the chicken all over with lemon and squeeze a few drops into the cavity, place in a snug-fitting saucepan, upside down and just barely cover with cold water. Add about two tablespoons of sherry, three teaspoons of Maldon salt, the carrots and onions roughly chopped, a bunch of bruised parsley stalks, a couple of bay leaves and a sprig of thyme. Bring to the boil and simmer very gently until cooked, about an hour. Remove the bird onto a dish. When cool enough take all the flesh off the bones and place in a nice serving dish. (Return all the skin and the bones to the stock and cook for a further hour; strain through a fine sieve and muslin; chill and then remove the fat.) Put the scraps and the leg meat in first, then good slices of the breast in an even layer on top. Moisten with four tablespoons of the stock. Cover the surface with foil and place weights on top. Leave overnight or for six hours. Meanwhile make a chicken liver pâté. Remove the stringy bits and any bile ducts from the livers and fry in half the butter for about three or four minutes, turning them over. Place them in a blender with a good grinding of black pepper, salt, the rest of the butter and a pinch of dried thyme, tarragon, marjoram and the clove of garlic. Pour three tablespoons of sherry into the juices in the pan, heat to bubbling point, then add to the livers. Blend to a paste, reserve in a little pot in the refrigerator. All this can be done a day ahead. When the chicken is pressed and chilled turn it out onto the foil and coat the base with half the liver pâté (keep the rest to eat at will), which I think is sufficient. Return the chicken to its dish, pâté side down. Now a chaud froid for the top covering.

Take three quarters of a pint of the stock and the half pint of cream, bring to boiling point in a saucepan, then simmer with a sprig of tarragon for ten minutes to reduce a little. Put the gelatine to soak in three tablespoons of sherry, when spongy add to the cream and stock off the heat and stir until completely dissolved. Adjust the seasoning, then allow to cool until the sauce has thickened and is starting to congeal. This can be hurried by cooling the pan over ice, but don't let it set. Spoon a layer of the sauce over the chicken and return to the refrigerator until set, repeat the process until all the sauce is used up. It sets very quickly on the chilled chicken. If you have had the dish in the chill for a long time, take it out a good half hour before eating, otherwise the flavours and texture are impaired, I think. Serve decorated with diamonds of cut tomato and perhaps a few choicely placed tarragon leaves. It should be accompanied by a rice and tomato salad. Simply boil the rice in plenty of salted water, drain and dress immediately with good olive oil and a tiny dash of tarragon vinegar, salt, pepper and a generous scraping of nutmeg. Have ready some skinned, sliced tomatoes already salted and peppered, slide them over the rice with their juices and leave until cold. Sprinkle with chopped chives, tarragon or parsley. You could also have a salad of green beans, french or broad, dressed in olive oil and lemon juice. A fine and exciting dish, I think. I cut it into wedges like a cake, getting a layer of everything.

1 July 1989

Use your Lammas loaf

I am so unnerved by the announcement that a bird-eating tarantula has given birth to 700 babies in London Zoo that my mind has glazed over and I can think of nothing else. What about next year when all those babies do the same thing? They are bound to get out or be let out by anti-something or other people, and life will be far more danger-ous than having attacks of lysteria hysteria. Any spider that can eat a bird is worthy of a lot of terror. However, on we must go. This coming Sunday, the first in August, is Lammas and – of the four agricultural festivals, Plough Sunday and Monday, Rogationtide, Lammas and the Harvest – it is the only one without secular customs. The name comes from 'Loaf-Mass', at which loaves of bread made from the first ripe corn were consecrated and offered to God. Seeing there is a new book on Lesley Blanch's excellent eating habits reminded me of a very useful picnic loaf of hers with which to celebrate Lammas.

——— Roquebrune tartine ———

1 long French loaf of the best quality garlic
10 ripe black olives
1 red pepper (pimento)
2 tomatoes

a handful of cooked green string beans
4 anchovies
2 tablespoons of olive oil
lemon juice.

Cut the loaf in half lengthwise, crush as much garlic as you fancy with a little salt and rub into the cut surfaces. Mash together the olives, the pimento thinly sliced, the tomatoes, green beans and the anchovies. Add the olive oil, lemon juice to taste and a good grinding of black pepper. When the mixture is thoroughly mixed, spread it on the loaf and sandwich the two sides together. Wrap in foil and put under a weighted pastry board for about an hour so that the flavours sink in.

Another use for the loaf is a splended beef sandwich which I once made for our previous editor Alexander Chancellor and his wife, who were driving to Italy; it lasted them all the way and remained moist and delicious to the end by all account.

──────── *Shooter's sandwich* ────────

1 sandwich loaf – the best you can   some big flat field mushrooms
  buy   salt and pepper.
1 thick rump steak

Cut off one end of the loaf then scoop out enough of the crumb to enable the beef and mushrooms to be introduced when ready. The rump steak should be about the size of the loaf's base and a good $1\frac{1}{2}$ to 2 inches thick. Grill the meat under or over a fierce heat, keeping it very rare. Remove from the heat and season on both sides with quite a lot of good sea salt and freshly ground pepper, then insert into the loaf. Grill enough mushrooms to cover the steak plentifully then push them into the loaf. Replace the deleted end of the loaf. Wrap the whole thing in a double sheet of clean white blotting paper and secure with string into a neat parcel, then secure again with grease-proof paper and more string. Place under a weighted board for at least six hours. When eating this sandwich just cut off each slice as required. 'With this "sandwich" and a flask of whisky-and-water a man may travel from Land's End to Quaker Oats [sic], and snap his fingers at both.' (T. Earle Welby, *The Dinner Knell*, Methuen, 1932.)

To finish on a sweeter note and with the markets full of very good peaches and raspberries I suggest you make this most beautiful and luscious of deserts.

——— [Cardinal peaches] ———
(Hume perhaps?)

10 ripe peaches
2½ pints water
1 lb granulated sugar

1 vanilla pod
1 lb raspberries
6–8oz granulated sugar

Put 1lb of sugar into a saucepan large enough to take the peaches, add the water and the vanilla pod, bring to the boil then simmer until the sugar is dissolved. Put the peaches into the syrup, bring back to simmering point and poach for eight minutes very gently. Let the peaches cool in the syrup for 20 minutes. Drain the peaches and peel while still warm. Place in a charming bowl and chill. (The syrup can be used to poach other fruits). Liquidise the raspberries and the rest of the sugar and if pip-fussy push through a sieve. Chill. When required, pour the raspberry purée over the peaches and decorate with mint leaves.

5 August 1989

We'll eat again

I might as well jump on the bandwagon of this 50th anniversary of the commencement of the late unpleasantness with everybody else. I recall the air raid sirens going off almost immediately war had been announced so we all sat under the stairwell waiting to be gassed at once and were rather amazed when nothing happened. The next day my mother bought several tins of soft herring roes and jars of olives as emergency food; we ate them within a week and that was that, nothing was ever stored again. But we did have a great bargaining power: tea. None of us drank it, having been brought up on sweet black coffee. Tea became gold-dust and coffee was never rationed.

Rations – an allowance of $\frac{1}{4}$ lb of butter, $\frac{1}{4}$ lb of bacon and $\frac{3}{4}$ lb of sugar, reduced to $\frac{1}{2}$ lb later on, red meat to the equivalent of a couple of chops a week, though offal was never rationed if you could find it, likewise poultry and fish; very little cheese unless you chose to register as a vegetarian. All this added up to a far healthier Britain, so we are told.

Free concentrated orange juice and cod-liver oil for the kiddies, who didn't like it, so the juice was often used to enliven gin which was itself pretty scarce, as were all such helpful beverages. We used to make mayonnaise with powdered egg, liquid paraffin and vinegar. We thought it marvellous at the time; can you imagine anything more revolting? This perhaps, to replace bacon for breakfast (everyone ate bacon for breakfast in those days).

Liver cake

½lb of liver (unspecified but probably ox)
6oz breadcrumbs
1 rasher bacon
1 onion

1 reconstituted egg
pinch of mace and allspice
a little chopped parsley
stock, salt and pepper

Mince the liver and bacon. Chop the onion finely. Mix all the ingredients together in a basin, bind with the egg and a little gravy or stock. Place in a greased basin, cover with greased paper and steam for 1½ to 2 hours. Allow to cool in the basin, putting a weight on the top. When cold, turn out and slice. This must be a pretty grisly sight on a bad morning, elephant grey I would think.

Here is another beauty from Gert and Daisy's wartime cookery book, price 6d. (3 pence). Gert and Daisy were Elsie and Doris Waters, a well-known radio comedy pair.

Faggots or *savoury ducks* or *Ducks with veils on*

"These are lovely served with pease pudding, and here's how to make them. Of course, you know the difference between faggots and sausages, don't you? (Answer: Sausages wear tights, while faggots flop about without any visible means of support)." *Daisy*

½lb pig's fry (any offal)
¼lb fat bacon scraps
4 large slices of stale bread
½lb onions
1 heaped teaspoon of chopped parsley

¼ teaspoon of mixed chopped herbs
pinch of mace (if you like)
pig's caul
salt and pepper

Soak the bread in water overnight. Squeeze dry. Wash and cut up the pig's fry. Cut up the onions and bacon and mix all well together with the salt and pepper, parsley, herbs and mace. Cut the caul into pieces and wrap a tablespoon of the mixture in each piece. Place joined side downwards in a baking tin or pie dish and bake in a hot oven for half to three-quarters of an hour.

Thank heavens Ruth Lowinsky came out with adapted receipts from her original *Lovely Food*. This is her wartime version of salmon soufflé, substituting tinned for real salmon, though even tinned salmon took up a lot of ration points and was a luxury item; dried eggs, margarine and milk take the place of eggs, butter and cream which would be considered much healthier by our nanny-state minders nowadays.

Salmon soufflé

½lb tin salmon
2 dried eggs

2 oz margarine
½ pint milk

Cook the salmon in its own liquid for a few minutes; pass through a sieve; mix the eggs, milk and margarine and add them to the salmon. (I imagine the margarine would have to be melted.) Put in a soufflé case and stand on ice before serving. Doesn't sound very appetising but there you are.

I spent most of the war at a convent in Hereford where we had delicious food cooked by French and Spanish lay sisters who knew about things like risotto, globe artichokes and salsify which they grew in the garden, none of which had ever been heard of by most of the rest of England. The only things I pined for were olives.

9 September 1989

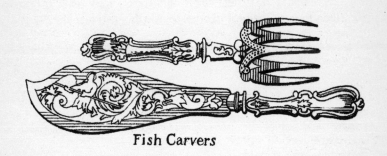

Fish Carvers

Sugar and spice

Michaelmas Day has passed us by, the feast of St Michael and all Angels when fat geese used to be eaten by the richer folk as the goose formed part of the Michaelmas rent. Ahead we have All Saints and All Souls – All Hallow's Eve on 31 October when children would go from door to door 'souling' for cakes or money by singing a song. If perchance you should be carving a pumpkin face for the occasion, here are some ideas for using up the inside.

When you have cut out the flesh, get rid of the seeds and the tougher fibres. The chunks can be roasted round a joint or added to casseroles and stews, but if you want a purée put them in a good heavy saucepan with a tiny amount of water, cover and cook gently until melting slightly, then turn up the heat to cook thoroughly and fast like making apple sauce.

Drain off the liquid and your purée is ready. Now make:

Pumpkin mousse

3 eggs, separated
4 oz caster sugar
1½ tablespoons cornflour
6 drops vanilla essence (not flavouring)
8 fluid oz scalded milk
2 tablespoons light rum
½ pint puréed cooked pumpkin

a good pinch each of ground cinnamon, cloves, nutmeg and ginger
3 fluid oz orange juice
1 tablespoon gelatine
1 pint thick cream
3 tablespoons icing sugar
slivers of crystallised ginger

Beat the egg yolks in a medium bowl until light; slowly beat in the caster sugar. Whisk in the cornflour and vanilla until smooth, then whisk in the scalded milk. Transfer the bowl to the top of a double boiler and cook over boiling water stirring constantly until the mixture is thick enough to coat a wooden spoon. Remove from the heat; stir in the rum.

Allow to cool, then mix in the pumpkin and all the spices. Put the orange juice in a small bowl and pour the gelatine evenly onto it; let it stand five minutes until spongy, then place the bowl over hot water until dissolved. Cool, then mix thoroughly into the pumpkin custard. Place the bowl into a larger bowl half filled with ice and stir with a wooden spoon until the mixture begins to thicken. Whip $\frac{1}{2}$ pint of the cream with two tablespoons of the icing sugar until stiff. Fold into the pumpkin mixture. Beat the egg whites until they form soft peaks and fold them into the mixture. Pour into a lovely dish or individual ones and chill covered for at least six hours or overnight. An hour before serving whip the rest of the cream and icing sugar and spread over the mousse. Decorate with slivers of crystallised ginger.

The other thing you should be making if you haven't already is the good old Christmas pudding.

―――――― *Christmas pudding* ――――――

1 oz blanched almonds	3 oz soft white breadcrumbs
1 oz glacé cherries	$\frac{1}{4}$ lb chopped suet
2 oz mixed peel	small pinch of salt
$\frac{1}{4}$ lb raisins	large pinch of mixed spice
6 oz currants	small pinch of freshly grated nutmeg
6 oz sultanas	1 small lemon
$\frac{1}{4}$ lb soft brown sugar	2 eggs
3 oz self-raising flour	6 tablespoons barley wine

This is for a $2\frac{1}{4}$-pint pudding basin.

Put a large pan of water to boil. Wash and dry the fruit unless prewashed. Roughly chop the almonds and cherries. Mix all the fruit and dry ingredients well together with the grated rind and juice of the lemon. Whisk the eggs lightly with the barley wine and stir into the dry ingredients. Mix thoroughly (giving each member of the family a stir for luck); if you are going to put coins in give them a good boil first. When all mixed, turn into a well greased pudding basin. Cut a square of foil (double thickness) two inches wider than the top of the basin. Make a pleat in the middle. Press edges under the rim of the basin, pleating as you go. To facilitate lifting the basin out of the hot water later, cut a double thickness of foil long enough to go under the basin and hang over the saucepan on both sides for handles. Lower the basin into the boiling water which should come threequarters of the way up the basin's side. Boil gently for six hours, topping up with boiling water periodically. Remove and cool, cover with more foil and keep until needed. Boil pudding for another two hours before eating.

7 October 1989

Charm the savage breasts

If music be the food of love we can celebrate its patron on 22 November, Saint Cecilia's day, though how she came to be chosen as such is rather a mystery. After describing the poor girl's martyrdom by roasting in a dry bath to no avail and then being partly beheaded by an incompetent executioner who left her to bleed to death for three days, Chaucer produced one couplet by which Cecilia's musical reputation must stand:

> And while the organs maden melodie
> To God allone in herté thus sang she.
>
> *The Second Nun's Tale*

However, by the Middle Ages she was well-established when the guilds of musicians adopted her as their patron saint, and with a few hiccups like the Reformation and the Puritans she has stood her ground. Mussels are meant to be a good food for love, so perhaps we should consume them for her feast.

This concoction was arrived at after I had bought a quantity of mussels and then found I had about a pint of vichyssoise left over in the refrigerator. I had no white wine, but did have a bottle of La Iña kindly sent to me by Simon & Schuster publications to accompany Elisabeth Luard's excellent little book about tapas. (Why are people advertising tapas bars? Bars have tapas, not the other way round.)

Mussels with Vichyssoise

For the vichyssoise:
6 good leeks
6 medium potatoes
2 oz unsalted butter

2 pints water or light chicken stock
6 fluid oz thick cream
salt and pepper

Slice the white part of the leeks very finely (you can use the green part as a perfectly satisfactory vegetable). Stew in a saucepan with the butter until softish then add the peeled potatoes, also finely sliced. Stir together and pour in the water or stock and about a dessertspoon of Maldon salt. Bring to the boil and simmer for 40 minutes. When cooled a little, whizz the whole lot in a blender. Leave to get cold, then stir in the cream. Check the seasoning and chill thoroughly for about six hours; serve in little bowls with a sprinkling of chives if so desired. This amount will be enough for eight people, so if you only have six you will have some left over for the mussels.

I reckon on a quart of mussels per person for a main course so this would be a healthy amount for two, or maybe three, at a pinch.

2 quarts mussels
a bunch spring onions
good handful parsley

5 fluid oz dry sherry or dry white wine
about 1 pint of vichyssoise

Buy your mussels in the morning if possible and leave to soak in cold water all day: this will ease the mud off. Discard any broken ones. Clean thoroughly under running water, removing beards and seaweed. Have a fine big saucepan at the ready and strew the bottom with the trimmed spring onions and the parsley, both finely chopped. Pour in the sherry or wine then pile the mussels on top. Cover with a well-fitting lid and set over a medium heat. Turn the shells from time to time until they are all open. Throw away any that firmly refuse to open. In a separate saucepan, heat the vichyssoise while the mussels are opening, then pour it all over them. Serve in big soup plates which have been well heated, and provide some good crusty bread.

A tasty dish from the tapas book and suitably in season:

Spiced pigeons

4 pigeons, cleaned and quartered
8 tablespoons olive oil
2 onions, chopped
16 fat garlic cloves, unpeeled

2 wine glasses dry sherry
1 tablespoon wine vinegar
2 bay leaves
salt and pepper

Heat the oil in a heavy casserole. Place the pigeon quarters therein and turn them in the hot oil. Add the chopped onions and the whole garlic cloves, fry for a moment or two. Pour in the sherry and the vinegar, season with salt and freshly ground black pepper, and tuck in the bay leaves. Bring to the boil, turn down the heat to a simmer, cover tightly and cook gently for 40 to 50 minutes until the pigeon pieces are quite tender. Towards the end remove the lid and evaporate all the juices leaving the pigeons bathed in aromatic oil.

Serve with bread, and make sure everyone has their fair share of the garlic cloves which will be creamy and mild-flavoured when slowly cooked like this. Pop them straight into your mouth from the papery coverings. Healthy and heavenly.

18 November 1989

Nottingham Jar.

Ducks trussed.

Larding Pins

Cheer fare

Advent starts next Sunday, rather late; it will only just manage to squeeze itself in before Christmas day. But before that we must not forget dear St Andrew or the Scots might be hurt. His feast, 30 November, is far more patriotically celebrated in Scotland than the weedy efforts made by the English on St George's day. A good traditional dish for St Andrew, apart from the usual whisky and haggis, comes from Jane Warren's *A feast of Scotland*:

──────── *Howtowdie with drappit eggs* ────────

3 lb roasting chicken
For stuffing:
3 oz fresh breadcrumbs
1 small onion, chopped
$\frac{1}{2}$ level teaspoon dried herbs (I would use fresh in larger quantities)
pinch of paprika
2 oz chopped ham
2 oz butter

4 oz butter
8 button onions
6 peppercorns
3 cloves
3 allspice berries
$\frac{1}{2}$ pint chicken stock
6 standard eggs
2 lbs spinach

Reserve the chicken's liver. Combine the stuffing ingredients, binding together with the butter. Place in the chicken and truss it. Melt the 4oz butter in a casserole, add the chicken and onions and let them brown all over. Add peppercorns, cloves, allspice, stock and salt to taste. Bring to the boil, cover and cook in a preheated oven at Gas 4, 350 °F, 180 °C, for 1–1$\frac{1}{4}$ hours until the bird is tender. Meanwhile cook the spinach, purée it, beat in a little thick cream and butter. Season. When the bird is cooked, strain the liquid into a saucepan and poach the liver in it for three minutes, leave on one side. Poach the eggs in the stock, then make six nests of spinach around the edge of a large dish, place an egg in the centre of each nest with the cooked chicken in the centre of the dish.

Rub the liver through a sieve into the stock, adjust seasoning, pour some over the chicken and serve the rest separately.

Now for Christmas I suggest you all make a good piece of dry-pickled, spiced beef to have up your sleeve. It is quite delicious and can be cut very thin, excellent with a baked potato and an endive salad. Straight from Dame David and Mr Hutton from Harrods.

——— *Spiced beef for Christmas* ———

10–13lb joint		5–6lb joint
	joint of fresh silverside beef	
5–6 oz	light brown Barbados sugar	3 oz
1 oz	saltpetre (from chemist)	$\frac{1}{2}$ oz
6 oz	sea or rock salt	4 oz
1 oz	allspice berries	$\frac{1}{2}$ oz
2 oz	black peppercorns	1 oz
2 oz	juniper berries	1 oz

Buy the meat in a long shape, without fat. Rub the beef all over with the brown sugar and leave for two days in a glazed stoneware receptacle. Crush the spices, saltpetre and salt in a mortar until well broken up. With this mixture you rub the beef thoroughly each day for 9 to 14 days according to which size you have chosen. Gradually with the salt and sugar the beef produces its own aromatic liquid. Keep it covered, in a cool airy place. Before cooking, wipe off any of the spices adhering to the beef. Put the joint into a deep cast-iron oval pot where it fits as snugly as possible with little space to spare. Pour in $\frac{1}{2}$ pint of water. Cover the pot with three layers of foil and its well fitting lid to avoid any evaporation of the juices. Bake in a very low oven at Gas 1, 290 °F, 143 °C, for five hours for a 5 to 6lb joint and, though the time isn't given for the larger joint, I imagine another hour and a half would suffice. Take it from the oven carefully and leave to cool for two to three hours, but pour off all the liquid before any fat sets. Wrap the beef in foil, place on a board, put another board or tray on top and a 3–4lb weight. Leave until next day. Once cooked, the meat will keep fresh for several days in a larder or refrigerator provided it is kept wrapped in clean greaseproof paper frequently changed between carvings.

If it has been stored in the refrigerator get it out for a good two hours before eating or the taste will be impaired. This joint must be cooked in a slow oven. It won't work on a slow burner above.

Harrods produces this meat beautifully but it costs £4 a pound whereas good silverside can be bought at under £2 a pound, so it is well worth taking the trouble. It would also be a different and interesting offering if you are staying with people for Christmas. So an early bon Nöel to you all.

2 December 1989

Freedom food

Plough Sunday and Plough Monday are the first ones after the twelfth day after Christmas, the feast of the Epiphany, but, as they moved the Epiphany on to 7 January this year, perhaps Plough Sunday is this coming one. Plough Monday was the day when work used to be resumed on the farm, emblematically at least, for no such serious work was attempted till Tuesday, such was the festive character of the day. I doubt if it is remembered anywhere nowadays and I'm sure no ploughs are brought to the church's chancel entrance any more. Perhaps in some of the recently freed countries they have kept up such customs in the rural areas where modernisation may not have encroached. As we will now be allowed to visit these forbidden countries, I thought a few of their receipts might be appropriate. Of all the Balkan people the Romanians were considered to have the sweetest tooth, but I shouldn't think the poor dears have had much chance to indulge it in recent years. More suitable, I think, is:

───── *Poor man's caviar* ─────

2 large aubergines	1 large onion
4 tablespoons olive oil	salt, pepper and paprika
2 tablespoons lemon juice	

Make sure the aubergines are firm and shiny. Put them on a baking tray and cook in a hot oven, Gas 7 to 8, 437 °F, 225 °C, until they are soft, about 45 minutes. Pierce with a skewer to make sure. When cool enough to handle, peel them and either mash the insides in a bowl or use a food processor; either way they must be absolutely smooth. Add the lemon juice, olive oil, salt and fresh-ground pepper to taste and about half a teaspoon of paprika, depending on whether it is the hot or the sweet one you prefer. Mix together thoroughly. Slice and chop the onion very finely indeed (you may prefer a Spanish onion, it being milder). Add to the aubergine mixture and chill until very cold. Serve as a first course with hot brown toast and butter and a few slices of thinly cut tomato. Caviar it ain't but it is very good.

My colleague James Knox and his wife have just returned from a joyous New Year in Budapest, so here is a Hungarian ham tart.

——— *Réteges sonkatorta* ———

1 lb boiled ham	2 tablespoons sour cream
1 white roll or large slice of bread	black pepper
8 fluid oz milk	1 lb puff pastry (home-made or
4 eggs, separated	bought)

Grind the ham very fine, preferably in a food processor or twice through a meat-grinder. Soak the roll or bread in the milk, squeeze it, then purée or sieve it. Add to the ham, together with the egg yolks, sour cream and a good grinding of black pepper. Beat the egg whites stiffly and fold into the ham mixture gently but thoroughly. Roll out two thirds of the pastry very thinly to line a 9″ × 2½″-high flan tin. Place the ham filling into the pastry-lined flan, roll out the rest of the pastry and cover the filling with it; make it fit the pan and pinch the edges together. Brush the top with a beaten egg and pierce with a sharp fork in a few places to allow the steam out. Bake in the middle of a preheated oven at Gas 6, 400 °F, 205 °C, for 50 minutes. This could be a first course for six to eight people or a main course with a salad for four.

12½ inches long 13s 6d each

No. 30 - CUCUMBER.

Another excellent dish, from Bucharest:

——— *Stuffed onions* ———

4 very large onions	butter
4 lambs' kidneys, chopped finely	olive oil
4 cloves	chopped parsley
nutmeg	salt and pepper
mixed dried herbs	

Get the largest onions you can find. Peel them carefully, we don't want them disingegrating. Place in boiling water to cook for 25 minutes. Remove from water and scoop out the centres with a clever little knife (a grapefruit one is handy), leaving about a $\frac{1}{2}''$ shell. Stuff each onion with a peeled, cored and chopped kidney. Add seasoning, one clove each, chopped parsley, a good pinch of nutmeg and mixed dry herbs. Put a lump of butter on each top. Stand the onions in an oiled, snug casserole where they just fit. Drizzle olive oil over them and more salt and pepper. Cover and bake for 45 minutes or until well done and soft in a medium oven, Gas 4, 355 °F, 179 °C.

13 January 1990

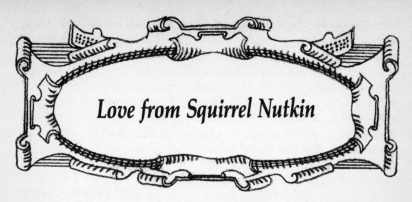

Love from Squirrel Nutkin

Dear old St Valentine is coming round again, but I think I have practically exhausted suitable heart-connotated dishes. The only new-to-me goodies I have found mentioned are Plum Shuttles or Valentine buns which used to be made in the now non-existent Rutland (such a blow when the ghastly powers that be mucked about with the counties; Rutland was particularly nice, being the smallest). Anyway these little oval buns were made in the form of a weaver's shuttle, full of currants and flavoured with caraway seeds to be eaten on St Valentine's day. If they are still being made I should be delighted to receive the receipt. All I can suggest for your delectation is a startling red risotto which I was served by Willie Landels last month. It is highly original, I should think, amazing to behold and most delicious, though it would make my lovely colleague, Clare Asquith, tremble with horror as she shies from beetroot as I do from spiders.

———— Ruby red risotto ————

3 medium-size cooked beetroots	1 medium-size onion
8 fluid oz milk	5 fluid oz red or white wine
$1\frac{1}{2}$ pints chicken or veal stock	$\frac{1}{2}$ lb arborio rice
olive oil	fresh parmesan cheese
butter	

Risotto is not a pilaf or anything to do with the dishes requiring that every grain of rice should be separate, it is therefore essential to use the arborio rice which has plump, succulent and absorbent grains. Buy the white grains, never the yellowish ones.

Put the beetroots and the milk in a blender, whizz until smooth. Have the stock heating in a pouring saucepan. In another saucepan put about two tablespoons of olive oil and an ounce of butter to melt. Peel and chop the onion very finely, add to the oil and cook gently until golden but not brown. Stir in the rice until it is well impregnated with the oil and butter, pour in the wine and let it continue to cook gently until absorbed. Now add a pint of the stock, cup by cup. Let it cook and absorb, but keep your eye on it, giving the odd stir, pour in the beetroot mixture and season with salt and freshly ground pepper. At the end of the cooking, which will be about 20 minutes, stir continuously to prevent sticking to the bottom of the pan and add the last of the stock if necessary. The rice should be a creamy consistency like a bowl of porridge but still have a slight bite to it. Add a tablespoon of freshly grated parmesan cheese, turn off the heat and let it rest for a couple of minutes, when it will be *'ben mantecato'* as the Italians put it. Serve at once with more parmesan on the side. This amount would be enough for four as a first course.

Sainsbury's, and doubtless other places, have been selling skinned turkey thighs lately, nice little hunks of meat which I find have far more flavour than the breast fillets. But you may prefer otherwise, so suit your own fancy. This is what I have done with the thigh pieces.

———— *Turkey thighs with pancetta* ————

2 pieces of turkey thighs each	olive oil
2 slices of pancetta per piece	chicken or game stock
juniper berries, bay leaf, sage	salt and pepper
madeira or medium sherry	

Let's say I am doing six pieces of thigh. Place them in a shallow dish, sprinkle with rock or sea salt and a good grinding of black pepper. Crumble a couple of bay leaves over the meat, about four fresh sage leaves or a large pinch of the dried ones. Dribble four or five tablespoons of the madeira or sherry over the top and anoint with two tablespoons of olive oil. Crush eight juniper berries and add to the marinade. Leave for about six hours or overnight, turning the turkey over every now and then. Buy the pancetta at your local Italian delicatessen. This is my answer to that horrible wet bacon we are served with nowadays. It is exactly the same cut of meat as streaky bacon, cured and sometimes smoked. We want the pancetta *'stesa'*; have it cut into thin slices. Wrap each turkey piece in two slices of the pancetta, making nice little parcels. Place them in a suitable oven dish, pour the marinade over them and put in a small amount of stock to cover the bottom of the dish. Place in a preheated oven at Gas 6, 400 °F, 205 °C, for 30 minutes, turning over at half time. Even better is to stuff each piece with a very lightly sautéed slice of turkey liver. Serve with glazed carrots, broccoli and purée of potatoes. Darn good.

10 February 1990

Amiable abstinence

I was delighted to see in last week's letters that they still bring the plough to the church on Plough sunday at Pevensey Church accompanied by a nice old prayer that the Greens might well take up as their motto. Many thanks to Anthony Hammond Christian (what a suitable name for the vicar).

Browsing through the estimable Jane Grigson's *Vegetable Book*, which I love and revere, I stumbled onto the sauce section and was reminded of the Greek version of ailloli which is traditionally eaten in Lent with slices of aubergine and courgette fritters or with beetroot and boiled potatoes. It is also excellent with boiled or fried fish. Made without egg-yolks, it is truly Lenten and non-salmonella-forming. Caterers, take note.

———— Skordalia ————

3 good fat cloves garlic
a 2-inch slice of stale white bread
   from a small loaf

3 to 4 oz blanched grated almonds
4 fluid oz olive oil
wine vinegar, salt

Crush the garlic well in a mortar or on a wooden board. Cut the crusts from the bread, soak the crumb in water, then squeeze out the

169

surplus. Add to the garlic in the mortar and pound away gradually, mixing in the grated almonds until you have a nice homogeneous mixture, then start adding the olive oil drop by drop to begin with, as for mayonnaise. Finally season with the salt and vinegar to your own taste.

Much as I love spaghetti con vongole (clams, cockles), I detest the grit that seems inseparable from those bought here, except for the very expensive tinned Italian ones. A great dish of pasta and mussels, however, is gritless and equally delicious. Mussels are fine and plentiful, so use them.

--------- *Maccheroncini with mussels* ---------

1½ lbs maccheroncini
2 large fresh tomatoes
1 tablespoon olive oil
4 lbs mussels in their shells

3 oz butter
1 onion, chopped finely
1 level tablespoon of plain flour
salt and pepper

Dip the tomatoes into boiling water for half a minute, peel, remove seeds and liquid. Chop the flesh finely. Clean and scrub the mussels, removing any beards and seaweed and discarding any that are broken or open. Put the oil in a large pan, then the mussels, cover with a lid and fry briskly until all the mussels are open. Take the mussels from their shells and keep on one side. Pass the liquid from the pan through a sieve lined with butter muslin and reserve. There should be a good half pint; if not, top up with boiling water. Gently fry the onion in the butter for two minutes, add the flour, and fry for another half minute. Add the mussel liquid little by little, stirring all the time until smooth; bring the whole lot to the boil, add the tomatoes, and season with salt and freshly ground pepper. Bring to the boil again and then simmer gently for a further 12 minutes. Now add the mussels for a moment, merely to heat through, then pour over the cooked maccheroncini, which you have drained into a warm serving dish. Mix well with two forks and serve. A good Lenten hors d'oeuvre would be the famous Mexican avocado mash:

Guacamole

2 tablespoons minced Spanish onions
1 small hot green pepper, de-seeded and minced
4 sprigs of fresh coriander leaves, finely chopped
2 good-size avocados

1 large tomato, de-seeded and chopped
2 tablespoons finely chopped red onion
1 tablespoon lime or lemon juice

When you de-seed the hot pepper and chop or mince it, wash your hands thoroughly afterwards — it's murder if you accidentally get it into your eyes. Mix the Spanish onion, the pepper and half the coriander with about $\frac{1}{4}$ teaspoon of salt in a mortar; pound into a paste. Into another bowl scoop the avocado flesh, but reserve the large stones. Mash well, then add the paste from the mortar. Mix thoroughly, stir in the tomatoes, red onions and the rest of the coriander. Embed the stones into the mixture (this stops discoloration) and sprinkle with the lime or lemon juice. Cover with cling-film and chill. Just before serving, remove the stones, give it a good stir and adjust seasoning

10 March 1990

INDEX